# THERE ARE NO
# ORDINARY
# PEOPLE

## Living as an everyday hero

# JEFF LUCAS

**CWR**

# Dedication

*To the lovely grandsons: Stanley and Alexander.*

*Live beautifully, boys, for and with Jesus.*

*That's success.*

# Acknowledgements

Thanks to my kind but ever-vigilant editor, Claire Musters. This is our second collaboration, and I hope it won't be the last.

I must acknowledge the team at CWR, who are Christians, and nice with it. I know, Christian and nice should always go together, but they don't, and so I'm grateful to the excellent team led by the unswervingly patient Lynette Brooks.

Most of all, I'm thankful to my Kay, for being *my* Kay for a lot of years, and for spending quite a lot of time being home alone while I tapped away in my study.

# Contents

# Preface:
## NOBODY IS ORDINARY (BUT NOT EVERYTHING IS AWESOME)

'My job as a mother is not to get my son in the top college, but to enjoy ordinary life. To swim in a pond on a hot day or walk with a friend or make dinner from scratch.' - Katrina Kenison[1]

'Give yourself permission to live an ordinary extraordinary life. Focus on your interactions with people in the now moment. At the grocery store. With your family. With your friends. Savor the king cake. Notice the softness of the cat. The dance of the leaves falling from the trees across the street.' - Carla Robertson[2]

'For the growing good of the world is partly dependent on unhistoric acts; and that things are not so ill with you and me as they might have been, is half owing to the number who lived faithfully a hidden life, and rest in unvisited tombs.' - George Eliot[3]

'We owe more to Barnabas than we often realize, Barnabas the son of encouragement. Where would Christianity have been without his marvellous gift for spotting and encouraging talent, for seeing the grace of God (and being glad!)? To him, under God, we owe the Gentile mission, and Mark, and even Paul. Thank God for Barnabas; and let him teach us to encourage one another.' - Dick France[4]

'I long to accomplish a great and noble task, but my chief duty is to accomplish humble tasks as though they were great and noble. The world is moved along, not only by the mighty shoves of its heroes, but also by the aggregate of the tiny pushes of each honest worker.' - Helen Keller[5]

'Barnabas ... Watch him! He is what God wishes every man and woman to be.' - Gordon MacDonald[6]

Please brace yourself. This could get ugly.

You're just a few seconds into this book, and I'm about to stain your mind with a most unhelpful mental image.

# I don't think I'd look that great in blue tights.

Despite my adolescent infatuation with Lois Lane, Superman I'll never be. He has taut, bulging muscles in places where I don't even have places. I've never been able to master the art of flying without tickets. In a casting audition, I'd be more likely to land the part of Superman's nerdy, bespectacled, bow-tied alter-ego, Clark Kent.

I'd love to saunter into a swanky cocktail lounge, armed and dressed to kill in an expensively tailored dinner suit. I'd introduce myself with those classic words, 'Bond. James Bond', and order a Martini that's shaken and definitely not stirred.

But it's never going to happen.

For one thing, I don't like Martinis.

And in a high-speed car chase, I'd probably end up with a flat tyre, waiting for a breakdown service, which would slow the action down somewhat.

I'd be pathetic in those fight scenes. With my precarious sense of balance, clambering along the roof of a speeding train would likely lead to a terminal tumble, especially if I had to wrestle a couple of thuggish giants as I clambered. Being allergic to pain, I'd never survive those lengthy punch ups: slap me lightly once and I'd sit down on the train roof, sulkily burst into tears and scream for my mother. Not very Bond-like.

And if the train happened to be hurtling towards a tunnel (it usually is), I'd forget to duck, which would result in a very radical haircut.

Even so, just one time, I'd love to be the guy who saves the day at the very last second – as the digital readout on the nuclear device counts down to zero. I'd snatch the earth from the jaws of disaster by neutralising the nukes or punching the errant meteorite, and then, just in time for cocktails, land up with the pretty girl on my arm.

But I'm not made of the right stuff to be a hero of the silver screen, never mind a superhero like Superman. All that sneaking around, maintaining a secret identity – not to mention having to slip into those clingy tights in the elbow-bruising confines of a phone box (remember those?) and maintaining a kryptonite-free diet – it's just not for me.

Okay, let's forget those mythical Hollywood heroes and superheroes. Aspiring to be like them is really rather silly, especially as they don't exist. But what about the real-life variety, the flesh and blood, extraordinarily heroic souls whose lives stand out as exclamation marks that punctuate history?

I wonder which faces materialise in your thoughts at the mention of the word hero?

Perhaps the name of Nobel Peace Prize winner Nelson Mandela quickly comes to mind. He endured eighteen years in Robben Island prison (out of a total of twenty-seven years of incarceration) refusing to bow before the jackboot of South African apartheid, and then became that nation's first black president. Often tagged as the 'Father of the nation', he was celebrated for his endurance, and esteemed for his graciousness and ability to reach out to all people.

While Mandela was still languishing in prison, Hendrik Verwoerd died. Verwoerd was one of the primary architects of apartheid. Incredibly, Verwoerd once described apartheid as a 'policy ... of good neighbourliness'.[7] He died at the hands of an assassin. Some time after Mandela was finally released, he visited Verwoerd's widow, Betsie. She received him with open arms in their house in a whites-only suburb: surely a beautiful portrait of reconciliation and grace. True heroism.

Or you might think of little Anne Frank, the diminutive Jewish girl who kept winsome hope alive while hiding from roving Nazi patrols in wartime Amsterdam. Aspiring to be a writer, the dark-haired teenager never knew that her diary would have such huge international impact, and become a literary classic. She perished, most likely from typhus, in Belsen concentration camp. The tragedy is compounded because she passed away in 1945, just weeks before Belsen was liberated by the allies. Named by *TIME* magazine as one of the most influential people of the twentieth century, she was described as a hero and an icon.

Then there are the brave, heroic souls who stared down impossible challenges and achieved the unthinkable, like Charles Lindbergh, the first man to fly solo and nonstop across the Atlantic. Bill Bryson, in his beautiful book *One Summer: America, 1927,*[8] chronicles the exploits of the shy Lindbergh, who became the most celebrated man on the planet in his time. Millions thronged the streets of New York to honour the awkward, reluctant aviator who was a genius flyer but somewhat clumsier when it came to social skills. He was also a flawed hero, and toppled from his pedestal because of an alleged unhealthy affinity with Nazism. The stunning achievements of his earlier life made him a true hero, nevertheless.

All of these were famous names, deservedly celebrated because they were head and shoulders above the crowd in their endurance, courage or gracious character.

But what of the rest of us, the 99.99 per cent of the human race who are not necessarily mediocre but are certainly relatively average - dare I say it, like you and me? What of those of us who might do quite well, but who don't excel, who will never see our names in lights, be serenaded by the sweet sound of applause or be told that we are amazing? What of us?

It's not that we wouldn't respond to an opportunity for classic heroism. We hope that, if faced with a crisis, we would show some mettle. But most of us won't ever be presented with an opportunity to rescue someone from a burning house, send that brute who is mugging the old lady packing, win the Wimbledon

Tennis Championships, fight an evil political system, score a goal in the World Cup or climb fearlessly through the so-called 'death zone' at the higher regions of Everest.

Can we be heroic in the world in which we live –
the world of the ordinary, the mostly humdrum?

Old Louis Armstrong was right. It's a wonderful world that we live in. But it's jammed with people who spend most of their days doing everyday stuff, which is, well, everyday.

Life is mainly run of the mill.

Vanilla.

Often boring.

Predictable.

Can we live heroically on a cloudy, drizzly Monday morning, as some of us steel ourselves for another journey on the tube, while others commit to the washing of a mountain of soiled nappies, or scour the newspapers yet again, searching for an elusive opportunity to be employed?

If we are even to have a stab at heroic living, perhaps we need to dispel a popular myth about life.

And that is that everything is awesome.

Really?

-       -       -       -       -

It's a word I've come to dislike intensely. I bristle when it's tossed around carelessly, like last night, when the server at a pizza restaurant used it to describe the calorific pepperoni slice that I ordered.

It's that word *awesome*.

The grinning waiter breathlessly affirmed my meal choice, enthusing that the pepperoni pizza was truly awesome.

I disagree.

It wasn't awesome. No way.

It was good, perfectly cooked, undeniably tasty and, because I was a little too generous when dusting it with chilli flakes, it literally moved me to tears on the first bite. But awesome it was not.

A recent popular children's movie included a catchy ditty that insisted that, when we stick together and act as a team, then everything is awesome.

But it's not true. Some of the best teams slog away when the task set before them is tiresome, tedious, back-breaking and even heartbreaking. Missionary Nancy Writebol of Charlotte, North Carolina, contracted the dreaded Ebola virus while working with Samaritan's Purse in Liberia. Being struck by that virus isn't an awesome experience – there were many times when she wondered if she would recover. Her faith in the midst of that trial was truly awesome.[9] But, obviously, the battle with the disease itself was a nightmare.

Perhaps awesome should be a reserved word, designated as a descriptor for only that which is genuinely epic. I know, beauty is in the eye of every beholder, but surely we could agree on a few sights that truly deserve the word awesome?

A brilliant orange sunset, slowly sizzling into the sea, setting fire to grey, utilitarian clouds.

Now that's awesome.

The impossibly tiny finger of a newborn, reaching out to discover what this new world feels like, and finding the hand of its mother – soft, warm, protective.

A usually stark field all dressed up for Christmas, blanketed with virgin snow, topped with a luxurious thick slab of whiteness.

The hand-holding veteran lovers who have just celebrated their seventieth wedding anniversary, and whose old eyes still glow for each other. Their knuckles are gnarly, but those hearts are still joined. Awesome.

Life is, for the most part, profoundly ordinary. Most of our days can be filed under the heading of 'not much happened'. This is not negative talk – it's just realistic.

For the follower of Jesus, there are red-letter days when, explosively or quietly, it seems that God is speaking, moving, intervening, orchestrating. Far from watching us 'from a distance', He is engaged with His world, and with us. But I'm not sure that He is as chatty as some would make Him out to be. Just as the biblical saints experienced flash points of life-altering experiences of the divine – and then years of rather ordinary life – so we too live in the wilderness that is a broken, sin-marred world. Occasionally a burning bush flares up quite unexpectedly, changing everything, but that's not a daily event.

# But I'm convinced that, in the midst of the ordinary, we *can* live extraordinary lives.

There are no ordinary people.

And it's not just that we are stunningly unique – although that's true enough, in that each and every one of us is fearfully and wonderfully made. A one-off. God doesn't have a production line, but makes irreplaceable people, breaks the mould and starts all over again.

And it isn't just that we have great potential. Too much talk of that banishes heroic living into the realm of some future, head-turning achievement and limits heroism to the sensational or exceptional.

But there are no ordinary people. Right now, without doing anything spectacular or epic, we can live beautifully and extraordinarily, by living ordinary life well.

And lest this begins to sound like hollow rhetoric from a hackneyed motivational speaker, that truth does not mean that we are all epically gifted, special or can achieve anything we aspire to. Let's be liberated from that lie, and the false promise it carries.

-       -       -       -       -

Some insist that everyone is special, amazing.

But we're not all amazing.

Such a blunt statement will be galling to those who insist that everyone is extraordinary, that school sports days should have no losers, only winners.

But when there are no losers, there are no real winners either. When excellence is so diluted to make it accessible to all, there's no authentic achievement.

To be told that we are all amazing, that we can do whatever we dream, is the stuff of Disney, not reality.

And when someone exposes the lie that's sold at graduation events, the line that's hawked around by those smooth-operating motivational speakers, it comes as a relief.

David McCullough, an English teacher, told graduating seniors of Wellesley High School in Massachusetts, 'You are not special. You are not exceptional.' His speech went viral:

> *In our unspoken but not so subtle Darwinian competition with one another – which springs, I think, from our fear of our own insignificance, a subset of our dread of mortality – we have of late ... to our detriment, come to love accolades more than genuine achievement. We have come to see them as the point – and we're happy to compromise standards, or ignore reality, if we suspect that's the quickest way, or only way, to have something to put on the mantelpiece, something to pose with, crow about, something with which to leverage ourselves into a better spot on the social totem pole.*[10]

In selling the lie, we place incredible performance pressure on children to always be top performers. When the dreaded Eleven Plus exam comes around (there are still areas in the UK that use it), when parents find out if their child is getting into the 'best' school: when young people take their exams, the pressure can be gargantuan.

It's not that we shouldn't inspire our children and each other to do our very best. But we are in danger of training young people to be instinctively disappointed with their achievements. We can drive them into thinking that life is all about public recognition and prizes, rather than relationships and special moments.

Pastor and author Kyle Worley is blunt:

> *Growing up in America, children consistently hear that they can 'be anything they want to be'. This promise is usually accompanied by thoughts of grandeur and extraordinary success. Our ambitions and hopes are educated on the premise that to settle for the ordinary,*

*which is often equated with what is boring and indicative of a past and inferior time, is beneath us. This hope of becoming something extraordinary trickles down from the rafters of our dreams, where we dwelt as children, into the basement of our hearts, where adults go to think about what could have been and prepare a path to projecting their fallen dreams onto their 'fallen' children.*[11]

For many, an ordinary life implies a meaningless life.

But the ordinary life lived well can be beautiful, and therefore should be celebrated.

The *Toronto Star* did just that in March 2012 when it printed a column about fifty-five-year-old Shelagh Gordon, who had recently died of a brain aneurysm. The headline ran, 'Shelagh was here – an ordinary, magical life'. The paper interviewed over one hundred people whose lives had been impacted by Ms Gordon – a woman who didn't have a great job, wasn't married and never had children. People would keep telling stories about her kindness.

The columnist commented: 'Shelagh Gordon is the perfect choice of an allegedly ordinary local woman whose life was actually huge in scope and as worthy of scrutiny as any big-life celebrity. She is you. She is us.'[12]

Everything isn't awesome. But life can be meaningful, as we live our ordinary lives in an extraordinary way. That way we can change the world.

–       –       –       –       –

Two thousand years ago lived a man called
Joseph (but usually called Barnabas).

His name is repeated no fewer than twenty-five times in the
book of Acts and five times in the epistles. I believe that he
played an absolutely vital role in the beginnings of the Early
Church. But you won't find a plethora of books about Barnabas.

Trust me, I've looked.

One scholar says of Barnabas:

> *Barnabas unfortunately now resides in 'undeserved*
> *obscurity', despite the fact that he 'played a substantial*
> *role in every stage of early Christianity and had a decisive*
> *influence on the fate of the church in the first century.'*[13]

Famous as an encourager, preachers tend to
introduce Barnabas to their congregations when
it's time to exhort them to be exhorters.

Beyond that, we don't tend to hear too much about him, and for
one very good reason: he falls under the substantial shadow of
his altogether more celebrated and famous apprentice, Paul.

And yet Barnabas was part of the small-core nucleus
of the Early Church, alongside Peter, Paul and
James. He is called a prophet and teacher (Acts 13:1),
an apostle (Acts 14:14) and one through whom God
worked miraculous signs and wonders (Acts 15:12).

Paul obviously became the first violinist in the kingdom
orchestra. Having occupied that first place for years,
Barnabas ultimately transitioned into playing second
fiddle, at least for a while – and ultimately, while Paul
blazed a trail that is carefully documented in the New
Testament, Barnabas' later ministry is not recorded.

Paul gave us most of the New Testament. Barnabas did not.

Although some believe that Barnabas wrote the epistle to the Hebrews, its authorship has long been a matter of dispute, and it seems unlikely that he penned it. Some believe that Barnabas wrote the 'Epistle of Barnabas', a letter to Gentile Christians urging them to abandon Jewish legalism, but that's very unlikely too. And the epistle didn't make it into the New Testament canon.

But, despite this, Barnabas made his mark by doing some very ordinary things, and living beautifully.

Probably unmarried, he gave himself selflessly to arduous travel in risky territories in order to fulfil his calling.

He believed the best about people, sometimes to a fault, and he defended the underdog even when it was unpopular and sometimes dangerous to do so.

He stood up for those whom others wrote off as failures.

Need someone trustworthy? Call on Barnabas.

He lived by his convictions, which is rare in today's society, sadly.

Looking for someone to cheer others on? He's your man.

How about a mission to sort out truth from error, in politically delicate circumstances, where the future of the entire Christian Church might be threatened?

Hopefully, without sounding like *Ghostbusters*, who are you going to call?

Barnabas.

That's not to say he didn't experience extraordinary episodes in his life.

Epic miracles.

Skirmishes with dark powers.

But his greatest impact came because he lived heroically in the midst of pressure, misunderstanding, tension and pain.

And so can we.

Me.

You.

There are no ordinary people.

-    -    -    -    -

*Do not ask your children*
*to strive for extraordinary lives.*
*Such striving may seem admirable,*
*but it is the way of foolishness.*
*Help them instead to find the wonder*
*and the marvel of an ordinary life.*
*Show them the joy of tasting*
*tomatoes, apples and pears.*
*Show them how to cry*
*when pets and people die.*
*Show them the infinite pleasure*
*in the touch of a hand.*
*And make the ordinary come alive for them.*
*The extraordinary will take care of itself.*[14]

# One:
## BECOME A SUPERMODEL

*'Joseph, a Levite from Cyprus' - Acts 4:36*

'Barnabas leads by example. His action shows a disciple of Jesus at his best.' - J.W. Packer[1]

'If you would convince a man that he does wrong, do right. But do not care to convince him. Men will believe what they see. Let them see.' - Henry David Thoreau[2]

'Worry not that your child listens to you; worry most that they watch you.' - Ronald Heifetz[3]

'"Very good, Jason Grace," Notus said. "You are a son of Jupiter, yet you have chosen your own path - as all the greatest demigods have done before you. You cannot control your parentage, but you *can* choose your legacy."' - Rick Riordan[4]

'A writer doesn't dream of riches and fame, though those things are nice. A true writer longs to leave behind a piece of themselves, something that withstands the test of time and is passed down for generations.' – C.K. Webb[5]

'I want the world to be better because I was here. I want my life, I want my work, my family, I want it to mean something ... if you are not making someone else's life better, then you're wasting your time.' – Will Smith[6]

'We are the Bibles the world is reading; We are the creeds the world is needing; We are the sermons the world is heeding.' – Billy Graham[7]

Barnabas never met this couple.

They lived in different eras.

But of this there is no doubt: his life affected their lives, and their deaths.

For those who stumbled upon the bodies it was a heartbreaking discovery, even though the young couple had been dead for so very long. He was only twenty-five, a man in the prime of life, and his wife was just nineteen. Victims of a cataclysmic earthquake, they had huddled together desperately as the ground convulsed beneath them. In vain, he had tried to shelter her from their collapsing house with his own body: his leg was straddled over her pelvis; his arm rested on her shoulder, perhaps a last gesture to try to reassure her.

Their last few moments were shared. As the floor churned and rocked, as walls and ceilings caved in, dropping tons of debris on them, they held hands as they died. History tells us that the terrible earthquake happened on 21 July, AD 365. A commentator from that period described the nightmare quake as 'a frightful disaster surpassing anything related either in legend or authentic history'.[8]

Hopefully their demise was swift and relatively painless. A modern post-mortem examination revealed that a large chunk of plaster hit that young wife's skull, snapping her neck at a right angle. But her husband took the brunt of the falling masonry, and his skull was crushed too. Seismologists have estimated that the quake probably only lasted twenty-five seconds or so, but it must have felt like an eternity.

There was worse to come for the archaeologists who made the grim find. Both husband and wife were cradling a tiny baby, the mother pressing her child's face close to her, nestled just beneath her chin.

They were followers of Jesus, these young lovers. In the dust and debris around their bodies a small bronze ring was found, probably the property of the woman. It was inscribed with the first two letters of the name Jesus Christ. And there were the letters Alpha and Omega, a cryptic declaration that He is the beginning and the end, the One who straddles eternity.

As their world came to such a violent end, they perished in the knowledge that though their dying must have been terrifying, it was not the end of the world - quite literally. While everything around them crumbled as the earth shuddered, this remained: their Saviour had beaten death, and so, ultimately, would they.

And this was their experience, partly because, over three centuries earlier, a couple of missionaries had arrived in Cyprus, bringing the good news of Jesus to the island.

But this intrepid missionary pair were more than just mere heralds, announcing a great new idea, espousing an alternative philosophy. Their lives had both been radically transformed by the Jesus whom they insisted was alive. Formerly local leaders, they were new to this type of work, inexperienced in mission, but they modelled their message well. The first was Saul (later known as Paul), and he had a friend and mentor with him.

Barnabas.

And for Barnabas, this was not new territory. He was back in his homeland, the place of his birth. He had news of a cross, an empty tomb and a kingdom, news that he would carry far and wide. But the first stop on his one and only missionary journey with Saul was home.

Cyprus.

-        -        -        -        -

Rome had been both good and bad news for the little Mediterranean island of Cyprus.

Formerly a part of the Greek empire, the island had been annexed by Rome for nearly a hundred years when Barnabas lived there.

Banish all thoughts of a primitive, isolated isle. The place was dubbed the 'Happy Island' by the locals. The gorgeous seaside city of Kourion was thriving, mushrooming towards a population of some 20,000 citizens. It boasted a massive stadium that had been in use for decades, constructed with walls twenty feet thick.

The Romans were quick to exploit the rich resources of silver, iron, copper, timber, corn and wine that were plentiful on the island. Money is a magnet, after all. The clusters of Jews that lived on Cyprus may have migrated there to do business. The island's copper mines had once supplied Herod the Great.

But all was not beautiful. The island was notorious for its licentious worship of Venus, or the Assyrian Astarte.

Although not the capital, the city of Salamis was the richest city on the island, and it became a favourite of later Roman emperors. There was plenty to entertain, with a theatre, gymnasium and baths. Stunning sculptures and intricate mosaics were in abundance. Here, a little Jewish family had lived, and the island had been kind to them.

Barnabas was born in the city of Salamis. His given name was Joseph, a common Jewish name. It was a name he would quickly lose, because he was destined to be given a new name by the apostles.

A member of the tribe of Levi, from which most Temple workers came, Barnabas had family members living back in Jerusalem. His aunt (some say sister) Mary and cousin (or nephew) John Mark (Col. 4:10) lived there. The Jerusalem-based family played a significant part in the life of the fledgling Church; Mary's substantial home was used for prayer gatherings (Acts 12:12) and she was well-to-do, affluent enough to be able to employ a servant. It seems that Barnabas' father had given up his rights and duties as a Levite and emigrated to the golden island – and perhaps then had moved back again to Jerusalem when Barnabas was quite young.

Barnabas was a man of means. As a Levite, he was not allowed to own land in Israel (although this tradition may have fallen into disuse), but had evidently become a landowner, most likely back in Cyprus.

In the first century, Levites had occupied a secondary role in the operation of the Temple, often serving as gatekeepers or enforcement officials. Prohibited from offering sacrifices and barred entrance to the holy place, they policed the Temple grounds and provided the music at sacrifices and on ceremonial occasions. As a Levite, Barnabas was fairly low in the Temple hierarchy, but still his role carried some status in the wider community.

Levites had not always just served in the background. Originally highly respected leaders, they were the oldest priestly caste in biblical history, and strongly associated with Moses and David. But times had changed, and these people, who had once held power, were forced to take a more supportive role.

This was Barnabas' background, although we're not told any further details of what being a Levite had meant for him.

# However, he was about to become a follower of Jesus.

And that decision launched him into a brand new life of incredible joy, surprising opportunities and relentless trouble too.

\-      \-      \-      \-      \-

There has been endless speculation about how Barnabas came to become a Christian. Some early traditions – not substantiated biblically – suggest that the young Cypriot had been schooled by the venerable Jewish Rabbi Gamaliel, and then met Jesus while in Jerusalem and became one of the original seventy-two who were sent out to declare the good news of the kingdom of God (Luke 10:1). The same tradition suggests that Barnabas won Mary and John Mark, those members of his wider Jerusalem family, as his first converts. There's even an unlikely tradition that Barnabas had tried, unsuccessfully, to convert another student of Gamaliel's, Saul, but Saul rebuffed Barnabas and his message and tragically became the architect of the persecution in Jerusalem that led to the martyrdom of Stephen. Of course, Saul eventually converted and became the apostle Paul, teaming up with Barnabas as he did. Still others say that Barnabas was present in the Upper Room on the day of Pentecost, but we have nothing to substantiate these ideas, biblically or otherwise.

And Dr Luke, who usually has an eagle eye for detail, doesn't help us when it comes to learning about Barnabas' background. He tells us nothing about his conversion experience. Perhaps there's a lesson here for us: what really matters is not how we come to Christ, be it in a sudden conversion or a growing love for God because we've been raised in a Christian home. It's not important how we *come* to Christ; what truly matters is that we do come to Him *then* follow Him. That's what Luke is more interested in.

From the way that Barnabas first appears in the biblical record, it seems that he was the first Levite to be won for the gospel by the apostles, reached immediately after the Sanhedrin had uttered its dire threats against Peter and John. If that's true, it means that Barnabas chose to follow Jesus when it was becoming increasingly dangerous to do so. The apostles would have been heartened to see a member of the Jewish establishment coming to faith. As a Levitical priest, he was the first of many to respond to the gospel. Soon others would follow in his footsteps: a 'large number of priests became obedient to the faith' (Acts 6:7). As we'll see, that's the way it usually turned out with Barnabas.

He was often the first one to step out, take the risk, blaze a trail – and then others followed.

# It was to be a pattern repeated through his life.

\-        \-        \-        \-        \-

As we'll be taking quite an extended journey with this man called Barnabas, perhaps it might help to consider what he looked like. And although Tom Cruise he was not, there's evidence to suggest he might have been quite the looker.

In ancient Christian art, Barnabas is often depicted as bearded. Sometimes he is painted holding a book or scroll of the Gospel of Matthew, a fellow Levite. And as a peacemaker and consummate networker, artists frequently have him holding out an olive branch. Because he spent so much time on the sea, travelling on his missions, sometimes he is depicted by the ocean. But how might we have any idea about what Barnabas really looked like?

There's a clue in the Bible about Barnabas' looks. Following a major miracle in Lystra, there was a case of mistaken identity:

> When the crowd saw what Paul had done, they shouted in the Lycaonian language, 'The gods have come down to us in human form!' Barnabas they called Zeus, and Paul they called Hermes because he was the chief speaker. The priest of Zeus, whose temple was just outside the city, brought bulls and wreaths to the city gates because he and the crowd wanted to offer sacrifices to them.
>
> (Acts 14:11-13)

Luke explains that Paul was mistaken for Hermes because of his oratorical skills – possibly suggesting that he was more noteworthy for his speaking than his looks. In early Christian writing, there is a physical description of Paul, describing him as 'a man small of stature, with a bald head and crooked legs, in a good state of body and eyebrows meeting and nose somewhat hooked, full of friendliness'.[9]

But Barnabas was tagged as Zeus, the supreme ruler of Mount Olympus. Middle-aged, but physically muscular and powerful, Zeus had an appearance that was both regal and commanding. Perhaps that *was* an apt description of Barnabas.

Handsome or not, and we can only speculate, what is certain is that Barnabas lived a beautiful life. He would never meet that little family who perished in the earthquake hundreds of years later, but, remarkably, he affected them. They lived and died in faith, partly because he had made such an impact on the island of Cyprus. He modelled the truth, which was then passed down through generations, and, as we'll see, we too are beneficiaries of his life and work.

# Barnabas was a man of legacy.

- - - - -

Legacy.

Superficially, the word can describe a sudden windfall of cash, or a hideous china ornament bequeathed by a loving but artistically misguided, departed one. In popular usage, we tend to think of legacy as something left behind when someone has gone. Or the legacy can be a value, a truth lived and handed on. Certainly Barnabas did that, championing grace when legalism was the prevailing notion.

# You and I both share in the grace legacy that his clear-minded courage bought.

But legacy is not just something we leave behind;
we can share it even as we live. As Marc Freedman
wrote in the *Harvard Business Review*:

> *Today, we can do more even than leave a
> legacy. We can actually live one.*[10]

Legacy is not just the influence through the
memory of someone past, but the healthy
influence of someone who is still with us.

Susan Bosak puts it like this:

> *The idea of legacy may remind us of death, but it's
> not about death. Being reminded of death is actually
> a good thing, because death informs life. It gives you
> a perspective on what's important. But legacy is really
> about life and living. It helps us decide the kind of life we
> want to live and the kind of world we want to live in.*[11]

Some legacies are intended as monuments to
human endeavour or philanthropy.

A hospital built or a scholarship created, and
then named after the benefactor.

The legacy honours their work, their life.

But the legacy that Barnabas gave us was never intended to
point us to him, but rather point us to the Christ who saved him.

# He was an example, a kingdom model.

Perhaps that's a partial explanation as to why, as we saw earlier,
Barnabas appears so suddenly, and with so little introduction,
in the book of Acts. Luke never really set out to write about

the acts of the *apostles*, but rather about the acts of the *Holy Spirit* at work through the apostles and the infant Church.

Luke offers us an achingly beautiful portrait of the shared life of those early disciples, describing a culture not just of giving generally, but specifically where believers sold land or property and donated the money to help those in need.

> *All the believers were one in heart and mind. No one claimed that any of their possessions was their own, but they shared everything they had. With great power the apostles continued to testify to the resurrection of the Lord Jesus. And God's grace was so powerfully at work in them all that there was no needy person among them. For from time to time those who owned land or houses sold them, brought the money from the sales and put it at the apostles' feet, and it was distributed to anyone who had need.*
>
> (Acts 4:32-35)

And then, as if to highlight one very specific example of what he's describing, Luke points the spotlight towards Barnabas (Acts 4:36-37). Out of many who gave, Barnabas was profiled as an example of selflessness and sharing. The idea of Barnabas being Luke's 'example' emerges in some translations more than others. In The Living Bible, Luke says 'For instance'. Other translations say 'so it happened that' or 'so it was with Joseph'.

Before giving us the chilling, negative example of hypocritical, posturing Ananias and Sapphira (Acts 5) – how not to do faith – he offers us the positive, shining example of the man from Cyprus. Contrasting positive and negative examples was a technique frequently used in ancient writing.

In short, Barnabas is one of Luke's kingdom supermodels, here modelling the kingdom not with great preaching, or by performing epic miracles, but by doing something ordinary: selling stuff, and freely giving cash.

-    -    -    -    -

The New Testament has plenty to say about the call to all of us to live exemplary lives.

Paul, Barnabas' companion, would later write about the power of following the example set by others, and didn't hesitate to nominate himself as a worthy example to follow:

> *Follow my example, as I follow the example of Christ.*
>
> (1 Cor. 11:1)

This is no 'do what I say, not what I do' approach to life, or a vague faith that cherishes orthodox notions and ideas on Sunday mornings, but then lives by a completely different agenda on Mondays.

Paul encouraged his young protégé Timothy to be an example to other believers 'in speech, in conduct, in love, in faith and in purity' (1 Tim. 4:12).

# And, of course, the greatest example of all was Jesus.

Refusing to settle for a nice sermonette about servanthood, He took a bowl and a towel, and washed sweaty, dirty feet.

> *Jesus knew that the Father had put all things under his power, and that he had come from God and was returning to God; so he got up from the meal, took off his outer clothing, and wrapped a towel round his waist. After that, he poured water into a basin and began to wash his disciples' feet, drying them with the towel that was wrapped round him.*

*He came to Simon Peter, who said to him,
'Lord, are you going to wash my feet?'
Jesus replied, 'You do not realise now what I
am doing, but later you will understand.'
'No,' said Peter, 'you shall never wash my feet.'
Jesus answered, 'Unless I wash you,
you have no part with me.'
'Then, Lord,' Simon Peter replied, 'not just my
feet but my hands and my head as well!'
Jesus answered, 'Those who have had a bath
need only to wash their feet; their whole body is
clean. And you are clean, though not every one of
you.' For he knew who was going to betray him, and
that was why he said not every one was clean.
When he had finished washing their feet, he put on his
clothes and returned to his place. 'Do you understand
what I have done for you?' he asked them. 'You call me
"Teacher" and "Lord", and rightly so, for that is what I am.
Now that I, your Lord and Teacher, have washed your feet,
you also should wash one another's feet. I have set you an
example that you should do as I have done for you. Very
truly I tell you, no servant is greater than his master, nor is
a messenger greater than the one who sent him. Now that
you know these things, you will be blessed if you do them.'*

(John 13:3-17)

And ultimately Jesus demonstrated what it means to
be a servant by walking towards a cruel cross.

Just as God raised a people, Israel, to be a beacon nation
to the earth, a working model of what life lived with
God looks like, then and now, we the Church are:

> *a chosen people, a royal priesthood, a holy nation, God's*
> *special possession, that you may declare the praises of him*
> *who called you out of darkness into his wonderful light.*
>
> (1 Pet. 2:9)

And this light shines, as day in, day out, we live ordinary lives well. 'Our critical day', said John Donne, 'is not the very day of our death, but the whole course of our life'.[12]

Years ago, when talking about faith, we would often say to enquirers (especially those who viewed the Church in a dim or disappointing light), 'don't look at us, look at Jesus'.

There are two major problems with that.

First, Jesus is currently invisible.

Secondly, God has designed things so that the world would be able to look at His people, and, in the looking, see the beauty and character of Jesus. The life of supermodelling is for all of us. J.R. Miller said:

> *There have been meetings of only a moment which*
> *have left impressions for life, for eternity. No one can*
> *understand that mysterious thing we call influence ...*
> *yet ... [every one] of us continually exerts influence,*
> *either to heal, to bless, to leave marks of beauty; or*
> *to wound, to hurt, to poison, to stain other lives.*[13]

And intriguingly, we are on display, not only to those around us, and to those without Christ, but to angels (and perhaps demons) as well.

Consider these verses:

> *We have been made a spectacle to the whole*
> *universe, to angels as well as to human beings.*
>
> (1 Cor. 4:9)

> *It was revealed to them that they were not serving*
> *themselves but you, when they spoke of the things*
> *that have now been told you by those who have*
> *preached the gospel to you by the Holy Spirit sent from*
> *heaven. Even angels long to look into these things.*
>
> (1 Pet. 1:12)

And then writing to the Ephesians, Paul says:

> *Through followers of Jesus like yourselves gathered*
> *in churches, this extraordinary plan of God is*
> *becoming known and talked about even among the*
> *angels! All this is proceeding along lines planned all*
> *along by God and then executed in Christ Jesus.*
>
> (Eph. 3:10-11, *The Message*)

When Paul mentions angels in Ephesians, he refers to both good and evil angels – angels and demons.

This is how God has chosen to reveal Himself, not only to the human race, but also to angels and demons in the invisible realm: through us.

John Stott puts it like this:

> *It is through the old creation (the universe) that God*
> *reveals his glory to humans; it is through the new creation*
> *(the church) that he reveals his wisdom to angels.*[14]

Know this: whatever your circumstances, Jesus has called you, together with all of His people at all times, to a lofty calling.

# Jesus wants me and you – us – to be supermodels.

Heaven, earth and maybe even hell are watching.

And there's nothing ordinary about that.

# Two:
# DON'T MAKE A NAME FOR YOURSELF

*'Joseph, a Levite from Cyprus, whom the apostles called Barnabas (which means "son of encouragement")' - Acts 4:36*

*'May our Lord Jesus Christ himself and God our Father, who loved us and by his grace gave us eternal encouragement and good hope, encourage your hearts and strengthen you in every good deed and word.' - 2 Thessalonians 2:16-17*

*'I long to see you so that I may impart to you some spiritual gift to make you strong - that is, that you and I may be mutually encouraged by each other's faith.' - Romans 1:11-12*

'Encouragement is oxygen to the soul.' - George Matthew Adams[1]

'One compliment can keep me going for a whole month.' - Mark Twain[2]

'People go farther than they thought they could when someone else thinks they can.' - John Maxwell[3]

'Sometimes our light goes out but is blown again into flame by an encounter with another human being. Each of us owes our deepest thanks to those who have rekindled this inner light.' – Albert Schweitzer[4]

Walt Disney, famous for that mouse and those magic kingdoms, said that there are just three types of people in the world. According to Walt, there are the well-poisoners. Gifted in draping others with wet blankets of discouragement, and obscenely eager to tell others what they can't do (even if they can), these vandals love to trample dreams and snuff out sparks of creativity.

Avoid the well-poisoners if you can, especially if you own a well.

Then there are the lawn-mowers. These are nice people, highly moral and meticulous, but they are exclusively concerned with their own lives, which includes, presumably, manicuring their lawns. They love their pristine gardens, fuss endlessly over them, but never move a muscle or lend a scythe to the guy next door so that he can chop his way through those chin-high weeds. If you're going to have an emergency, pray it doesn't happen on a lawn-mower's doorstep. They won't be in.

Finally, in Disney's experience, there are the life-enhancers. These beautiful souls are quick to reach out, and live with their eyes and hearts open. Fuelled by a passion to strengthen and enrich others, the life-enhancers encourage, lift up and inspire.

Before Barnabas was called as an apostle, before he became a sponsor of and co-worker with Saul/Paul, before he worked any miracles and even before he became a generous donor to the community welfare fund of the Jerusalem

church, he was a life-enhancer, or, to use language that
Dr Luke would be more comfortable with, an encourager.

# If encouraging was an Olympic sport, Barnabas would have been a champion.

But he got a better award.

He was dubbed with a new name, a nickname
– one that suggested, tongue-in-cheek, that his
father was a chap called encouragement.

Luke introduces this man to us as a consummate encourager.
Perhaps countless small acts of kindness, exhortation, empathy
and selflessness earned him the reputation, and so the name.

He didn't make a name for himself; others made it for him.
Goodbye Joseph. Hello Barnabas.

-        -        -        -        -

In my youth, I did have a very odd nickname. As an
enthusiastic member of the local Army Cadet Force,
I was nicknamed after a part of a gun.

Seriously.

The self-loading rifle (or SLR) has a metallic component
beneath the barrel called the gas plug. I have a somewhat
indented nose; a deviated septum. And so I was tagged,
'Groove in the Gas Plug' because I am blessed with a beak
that apparently looks like the end of a dangerous weapon.

Name-calling of a far more affirming kind occurred in
the Early Church. In fact, throughout history, God has
frequently handed out new names and nicknames.

Abram became Abraham, and elderly, barren Sarai blossomed impossibly as pregnant Sarah.

Jacob became Israel. Jedediah became Solomon.

Jesus renamed fisherman Simon as Cephas, or Peter, the rock.

And Jesus gave James and John a joint nickname, one that would make a motorcycle gang proud: the sons of thunder.

Later, after he fell off his high horse, persecutor Saul had a name change too, and became the apostle Paul.

So what does Barnabas mean? As we've seen, Dr Luke, writing primarily for his Gentile audience, translates the word to simply mean 'son of encouragement'.

The Greek word Luke uses has 'exhortation' as a part of the meaning, and the word *paraclete* is a component of the name too – the very same word that is used of the Holy Spirit, the 'comforter', or the one who draws alongside. And there's yet another aspect to Barnabas' name, which has to do with being prophetic. It may be that Barnabas brought encouragement through his preaching as well as his personal interaction with people.

Put all of this together, and a rather beautiful definition of encouragement emerges.

*Exhortation*: stirring others to achievement and excellence, through word and example.

*Drawing alongside*: not merely speaking at people, but standing shoulder to shoulder with them, incarnating ourselves into their lives.

*Prophetic*: consciously or unwittingly bringing something of the heart of God to others as we encourage.

Barnabas. It's a wonderful name, and not least
because of a vital but often overlooked truth.

# When we encourage,
# we're quite like God.

-     -     -     -     -

Superlative as he was as a life-enhancer, Barnabas
is not the Bible's most encouraging character.
That epithet belongs to God alone.

Paul writes to the Romans, and celebrates 'the God
who gives endurance and encouragement' (Rom. 15:5).
His prayer for his friends in the Thessalonian church
reveals the same Lord who cheers us on:

> *May our Lord Jesus Christ himself and God our*
> *Father, who loved us and by his grace gave us eternal*
> *encouragement and good hope, encourage your hearts*
> *and strengthen you in every good deed and word.*
>
> (2 Thess. 2:16-17)

'Good hope' is a phrase that was commonly used in Paul's
day to refer to life after death, and so Paul's logic is this:
God will be encouraging us throughout eternity, and so
that very same God wants to encourage us today.

And in Paul's thinking, encouragement and strength are linked
– the words often appear together in the New Testament.
Christians aren't strengthened by brow-beating, harassing
teaching that seeks to scare them into action. Rather they
are lifted up by God's encouragement and galvanised
by words of blessing. Encouragement is great fuel.

Many of us struggle to picture a God who is delighted by our efforts, who cheers us on and who is the ultimate source of all strength and encouragement. The notion of an encouraging God seems almost too good to be true. And some of us live tortured lives because our view of God is anything but encouraging. He is the relentless taskmaster, never satisfied, always demanding more, no matter how hard we work or what sacrifices we make. We call Him Father, but respond to Him as if He is a tyrant. Perhaps this twisted picture of God has been formed in us by our upbringing, or comes as the result of our sitting under harsh, brutal preaching. Some of us have been bruised or abused by earthly fathers, so the idea of a loving, encouraging God seems impossible for us to grasp. If that is our history, let's remember that Scripture never teaches that God is like a human father; on the contrary, Jesus teaches us that our Father in heaven is quite unlike any father we've ever known:

> *If you, then, though you are evil, know how to give*
> *good gifts to your children, how much more will your*
> *Father in heaven give good gifts to those who ask him!*
>
> (Matt. 7:11)

The alphabet of Christianity begins with 'F' for father. Without that knowledge, we will live fearful, breathless, manic lives. God is the greatest encourager in history. Yet much of the time, He channels that encouragement through human conduits.

That would be us.

# And that's where the blockage often happens.

- - - - -

It's a rather strange phenomenon that happens frequently in my life. When I go through a time of emotional turbulence, or get exhausted due to the demands of ministry (or more specifically because of my mad scheduling), an email of encouragement arrives, a card of appreciation is delivered or a life-giving conversation is shared. Just last Sunday a man approached me after I'd preached at a church that I visit regularly, and his words made a deep impact on me: 'Whenever you speak, Jeff, we feel that you're on our side. You want to nudge us forward, but never make us feel like you're not one of us - rather, we sense that you're with us.'

That sentence probably took that kind man less than thirty seconds to say, but his words strengthened me all week, and warm my heart again now as I recall them.

Paul celebrated the encouraging God, but he often received encouragement and refreshment through veteran, faithful friends. Sadly, too often we are hesitant to bless each other with encouragement, fearing that we might be thought of as flatterers, or that we risk inflating the ego of the one we're encouraging, which is rarely the case. Most of us are painfully well aware of our fragilities and flaws, and encouragement strengthens our hearts rather than inflates our egos.

Barnabas might have been naturally blessed with a warm, sunny personality.

But what of those who insist that being encouraging is not part of their natural disposition?

Some people are natural encouragers, and they do it without much apparent effort. And then there are those that Paul referred to when he described encouragement as a 'gift', writing to his friends in Rome (see Rom. 12:6-8). Perhaps Paul was expanding on the role of a teacher who informs and encourages as they fulfil their gift, but it may be that some are not only naturally inclined to bring strength through encouragement to others, but are gifted by the Holy Spirit to do so.

But there's a danger that we use that idea to excuse ourselves, insisting that we are not shaped temperamentally or gifted charismatically to bring comfort and encouragement.

And that's a poor excuse.

I've even seen grim-faced souls who not only rarely encourage, but apparently believe that God has called and gifted them to do the opposite, as they constantly complain and critique as self-appointed 'watchmen and women' in the Church. Whatever our personality type, we should know that encouragement is commanded of all of us. Paul was a master encourager despite finding himself in some very difficult circumstances, such as imprisonment and persecution. Rather than retreating into introverted 'bless me' mode, he encouraged others even though his own life was so incredibly difficult.

# Encouragement is obedience.

And it should be mutually shared, too.

It can happen in congregations, in families, in friendship and in marriages – encouragement becomes something that a person tends to take, but never give. The blessing of encouragement becomes a one-way street, and ultimately the person assumes a posture of being a permanent victim, always in need, always wanting others to build them up, but never returning the favour. Sometimes we find ourselves in a place where life is so hard that we don't feel we have the energy to encourage others, but we continue to crave their help and support. Ultimately, that attitude, in which we become a sponge rather than a conduit, is likely to damage any relationship, no matter how committed.

And encouragement is strategic too. The writer to the Hebrews makes it clear that encouragement is not always a spontaneous, spur-of-the-moment action, but often comes as a result of careful consideration:

> *let us consider how we may spur one another*
> *on towards love and good deeds*
>
> (Heb. 10:24)

'People who add value to others almost always do so *intentionally*. I say that because adding value to others requires a person to give of himself, and that rarely occurs by accident' writes John Maxwell.[5] And the writer to the Hebrews calls for encouragement with purpose – not just to create a feel-good factor, but to spur one another on to greater love and good deeds. The word *spur* here is a fairly strong word, suggesting that with our encouragement we prod and stir each other on to greatness. When we carefully write a note of well-phrased thanks, or express very specific and thoughtful appreciation for the service that others have done for us, we nudge them on to even greater things. Don't just pat someone on the back and say 'well done', but rather tell them *why* what they did was done well. Let's help each other, not out, but up.

In Timberline Church, we have tried to adopt encouragement as one of our core values, seeking wherever we can to 'catch people doing something right', and honouring and encouraging them as we do.

# Let's be sure that, if our encouragement is planned, it's authentic too.

Thoughtless encouragement is not terribly useful – on the contrary. When people see that encouragement is the standard fodder - dished out even to those who haven't actually done well, just to try to make them feel better - it soon becomes like a devalued currency. When warm words are tossed around so freely they flatter rather than encourage, they lose any impact and everyone becomes suspicious about their authenticity. A friend of mine recently said, 'I don't want to be encouraged, I want to have feedback - to know what I've not done so well, as well as know where I've succeeded.'

And sometimes, as Barnabas would discover (at great cost), encouragement includes conflict, even rebuke.

Because God is the Lord of encouragement doesn't mean that everything He does will be easy for us, or that He only speaks words that are pleasing to hear. There will be times when God will bring discipline into our lives, not because He doesn't love us, but because He loves us so much. God's encouragement to us is that we are His children - sons and daughters of the living God. Discipline is only given by a parent to children who are deeply loved and cared about - and that, with God, includes us. And so encouragement is not just about warm words shared; rather, encouragement may include confronting each other. Paul instructed Timothy to 'rebuke and encourage' (2 Tim. 4:2), which not only suggests that a rebuke should always be accompanied with encouragement, but also that strong words might be vital if we are to be saved from ourselves.

This isn't easy to live out. I've discovered that it's not enough to ask a few trusted friends to tell me if they think I'm going wrong; it's as if I need to ask them in nine different ways, and put my request in writing if I'm genuinely to allow them to tell me what I don't want to hear. And I need to ensure that if they do come with a word of correction of rebuke, I won't react in a defensive or hostile way that will guarantee they'll never do it again! Looking back over my Christian journey, I know I could have been spared a lot of heartache if I'd not only asked my closest friends what they thought, but really impressed upon them that I wanted them to speak the truth.

Encouragers are willing to point out what's wrong as well as commend what's right.

- - - - -

As we'll see as we continue to reflect on the remarkable man that Barnabas was, encouragement was a consistent thread in his life. We'll look at those other episodes in detail later, but for now, let's affirm just how consistent he was at building others up.

He was the encourager with a field to sell, and a gift to give.

He travelled to Antioch and specifically encouraged the new Christians there.

He refused to succumb to fear, and encouraged the newly converted Saul by vouching for him in Jerusalem, and initiating a warm welcome.

Saul received encouragement again when Barnabas went looking for him, located him in Tarsus and opened a ministry opportunity for him, again, back in Antioch.

He encouraged John Mark by standing with him and remaining loyal, even though Mark had failed.

Today, all around us, there are people who are weary, hungry for some hope, desperate for some encouragement.

Truett Cathy sums up the dire need we all have of encouragement: 'How do you identify someone who needs encouragement? That person is breathing.'[6]

If we are willing and intentional about being deliberately aware of others, looking beyond the demands of our day and the tasks we have to accomplish, and offer ourselves to God, then we might just bring a life-changing word of encouragement to someone this very day.

Dr Larry Crabb said:

> *Encouragement is not a technique to be mastered;*
> *it is a sensitivity to people and a confidence in God*
> *that must be nourished and demonstrated.*[7]

So let's go ahead and make someone's day.

And perhaps as we do, we will discover that, like Barnabas, we don't have to make a name for ourselves, but someone else will dub us with a beautiful nickname.

# Three:
## GIVE UP

*'Barnabas ... sold a field he owned and brought the money and put it at the apostles' feet.' - Acts 4:36-37*

*'A generous person will prosper; whoever refreshes others will be refreshed.' - Proverbs 11:25*

'It is possible that Barnabas' gift represented a considerable amount. Perhaps his field came from the rich fruit-growing lands of Cyprus ... if so, his land probably was worth more than a stony field in Palestine.' - Robin Gallaher Branch[1]

'The cold within him froze his old features, nipped his pointed nose ... made his eyes red, his thin lips blue; and [he] spoke out shrewdly in his grating voice.' - Charles Dickens[2]

'True generosity doesn't stop with possessions. It starts with them.' - Chip Ingram[3]

'Profound conversion of heart produces generosity.' - Gordon MacDonald[4]

'No act of kindness, however small,
is ever wasted.' - Aesop[5]

It's a question that every Christian has asked at some point.

# We know our world is broken. But is it beyond repair?

Faith responds to the question with yet another
question: is anything too hard for the Lord?

A shrivelled womb carries Isaac.

A sea parts obediently at the wave of a rod
(that is occasionally a snake).

A bolt out of the blue consumes Elijah's sacrifice atop Carmel.

Vintage-tasting wine comes from water,
aged to perfection in a second.

Cloudy eyes, blind from birth, suddenly clear and focus.

For a synagogue leader's daughter, death is sent
packing. A pulse is unexpectedly detected.

Previously stinking Lazarus shows up for lunch.

Is anything too hard for the Lord?

The broken body of an executed man comes to life again,
three days after His death - confirmed by many witnesses.

A hurriedly borrowed tomb is vacated.

# With God, all things are possible.

When it comes to the question, 'can the world
be changed?' we know that God can do it.

The challenge is more specific. How might He do it?

We believe we have a message, *the* message,
that can truly revolutionise the world.

So what's it going to take to cause our busy, technology-
distracted culture to at least stop and listen for a while?

Some answer the question with just one word.

Revival.

We need a revival, they say, a sovereign move of God that
will shake communities and nations to the core. They point
to the Azusa Street revival of 1906, when a black, one-eyed
preacher called William J. Seymour gathered huge crowds and,
according to some, shook the city of Los Angeles. There were
reports of miraculous healings and people speaking in tongues.
Not only that, but in a segregated America where women
still didn't have the right to vote, women were encouraged
in leadership, and the congregation was multi-racial.

Around the world today, half a billion Pentecostals
view the Azusa Street gatherings as the birthplace
of the modern Pentecostal movement.

But even if revival is what we need (and that is not our primary
subject here), at the very least we need to ask some serious
questions about what constitutes revival because, in our thirst
for the spectacular and our genuine hunger to see our world
changed, we can engage in an unseemly haste, breathlessly
announcing revival when perhaps something else is happening.

In the last few decades, I've heard of a number of revivals,
which usually look like this:

Something spectacular happens somewhere,
like a remarkable, authentic healing.

Interested crowds gather.

Expectation is high, the atmosphere is exciting, electric even.

Crowds beget crowds. People buy plane tickets. More crowds.

The presence of so many causes some to announce that
a revival is happening. And that brings more crowds ...

I'm not sure what revival is, and if we should be
seeking it, but I don't think that a large group of
undeniably enthusiastic Christians (with a few interested
pagans showing up too) constitutes a revival.

In New Testament history, the arrival of the gospel
shook entire cities. Local power players trembled. People
gathered in stadiums, screamed threats of lynching
and the peace was very much disturbed because their
economy was being affected. Many turned from their
fascinations with the occult; books were burned; those
who traded in magic trinkets got very upset indeed.

The faithful souls who were key in biblical revivals
usually became fugitives, not lauded celebrities.

If revival is what we need, then, at the very least, we must
not allow our hope of it to sanction laziness about what
we are called to do to grab the world's attention. Revival is
a word that can be used as a trump card to allow us to be
reluctant to reflect about what we should do, because all
of our hope is centred on what God might possibly do.

And then there are those who insist that signs and wonders
will turn the heads and the hearts of our generally
indifferent culture, and, in a sense, they're right.

The Early Church was a miraculous Church. Stunning signs and wonders were a regular feature of Barnabas and Saul's apostolic travels. But I'd like to suggest that it took more than a miracle to turn a culture.

Others would suggest that we need yet more evangelistic campaigns, co-ordinated missions. And perhaps they're right too, although, at the risk of sounding churlish, my experience is that they generally promise more than they deliver.

Consider the Early Church.

They did change the world.

## They saw miracles, but had no Facebook page to post the photographs on.

They had no structure to support their growth, no carefully co-ordinated marketing campaign, game plan, or for that matter, any other plan.

And then they were living under huge pressure, which could have stifled their growth. A psychopath called Nero was waiting in the wings, so that within thirty years of the resurrection of Jesus, government-sanctioned persecution would kick in – a shadow that would fall over the Church for 300 dark years.

Andy Stanley sums up their predicament:

> First-century Christians weren't organized, had no buildings, and weren't recognized by the government. In everyday society, they were basically considered a cult. For nearly three centuries, they remained utterly powerless – ostracized socially, persecuted politically, and tortured physically. And yet somehow their movement continued to grow.

*How do you explain that?*

*Over the years, a number of historians have explored this phenomenon in detail. People such as Rodney Stark, Paul Johnson, and Alvin Schmidt have dedicated much of their careers to understanding how Christianity could not only survive but actually thrive. Their conclusion is nothing short of remarkable.*

*While Christianity had none of the conventional strengths required to start a movement, its appeal and influence can be traced to an unexpected source: generosity.*

*The hallmark of Christians in the first century was not their wealth. They had none. It was not their theology either. Their beliefs were so odd, religious people couldn't understand them. What gave them leverage was their inexplicable compassion and generosity. They had little, but they gave. They received little compassion, but they were willing to extend what they had to other people. They were impossible to ignore.[6]*

Those early Christians gave. They gave their service, their money, their goods, their time, their safety, their creature comforts, their reputations. They gave to their own, but not just to their own. One emperor, Julian, described the followers of Jesus as 'impious Galileans [who] not only feed their own poor but, ours also'.[7]

# Generosity for them was not just a series of isolated, unusual actions, but was their way of life.

They were different.

Centuries earlier, the philosopher Plato had advocated the idea of generosity, but it was an idea whose time had not come. And then came the Christians, living in a culture where something called *liberalitas* was practised.

*Liberalitas* worked well if you were a person of means. Simply put, the code went like this: you scratch my back, I'll scratch yours. I'll give to you, because one day I'll call in the note, and you'll owe me. Giving was investment. A tidy arrangement, that is unless you were poor and had nothing to give.[8]

And so if you had nothing, you weren't of much use. You'd be left outside in the cold. So strong was this thinking in the culture, that even Jewish practice mirrored it. The poor stayed poor. Widows and orphans stayed at the bottom of the social food chain.

But the followers of Jesus took Him at His word. They scattered good everywhere, freely, indiscriminately. They had no expectation of payback. They loved the unlovely. Crossed over the street, like Good Samaritans.

# They rewrote the textbook on how to be a good neighbour.

They looked for sweaty feet to wash, and even went further. When terrible plagues hit, and huge swathes of the population fled the cities, abandoning the sick, the Christians stayed behind, nursing the ill back to life - which meant that some of the carers died in the process. And this was no holy huddle. When pagan priests fled, the Christians cared for the sick pagans, many of whom converted to Christ, unsurprisingly.

Stanley describes their courageous compassion:

> *They weren't afraid of death. As they nursed the sick back to health, word of their generosity spread like wildfire.*[9]

They didn't just give out, they gave up,
as an act of worship to God.

They were a sign and a wonder to a wondering world.

Gordon MacDonald writes:

> In a heartless world, the generosity and service of
> the first Christian generations was such a stunning
> contrast that people everywhere sat up and took
> notice. It is fair to speculate that Christian generosity
> and service did more to win people to the gospel
> of Christ than all the preaching that was done.[10]

That's just what generous people do. They change the
world, by showing the world what God looks like – and He
is the ultimate giver. We are most like God when we give.

The world takes notice of givers.

That's what we need. To stand out. Be distinct. Be
known as different, not just because of what we
don't do, but because of the way we live.

I'll say it again.

# The world takes notice of givers.

I have heard it said recently that generosity
is 'the new evangelism'. But there's nothing
new about it: it's the old, original way.

And in that ancient Church of givers, there was one
man who stood out. In writing Acts, Dr Luke selected
one man who exemplified the spirit of generosity.

Yes, you got it in one.

That would be Barnabas.

–        –        –        –        –

It's not just that Barnabas gave; he gave
sacrificially and generously.

Luke doesn't tell us the specific amount of money
Barnabas gave but what we do know is that selling his
field and donating the proceeds would have cost him
dearly. Later he, together with Paul, would have to work
for his living to support their apostolic travels (1 Cor. 9:6).
Perhaps if he had held on to that property, he could have
lived off of the investment later in life and ministry.

But, prompted by the need and nudged by the Spirit, he gave.

And his giving would have also cost him in time and
effort. I don't know what was involved in buying and
selling property back then, but suffice to say facilities for
the electronic transfer of funds were not available. It's
highly likely that it was a lengthy and tiring process.

# Generosity takes work, strategy and effort.

We need to think, talk and pray about our regular
giving. Take time to consider the work of a charity
you are considering supporting. Be intentional.

And then Barnabas abandoned control as he gave. There
were no strings attached. He placed the money at the
apostles' feet and, in so doing, was generous with trust,
believing that they would do what was right with the gift.

That's not to say that we don't need stringent economic
accountability in the Church. I'm increasingly nervous about
large churches where senior leaders have total discretion over
pots of money, to use as they see fit. But, while leadership

must always be fully accountable to the wider Church in the way that finances are managed, there's a danger that those who give greatly demand more control over the way that money is spent. When that happens, the gift becomes a curse rather than a blessing, because a controller has been created – and soon there will be tears. That obviously doesn't rule out appropriately designated gifts, but it means that when we give, we should do so with an attitude of trust and a willingness to be open-handed and open-hearted in our giving.

And then open-handedness in giving should mean that we're not dependent upon a specific response from those who benefit from our generosity. Sometimes we lose the joy of giving because we harness ourselves too closely to the responses of those to whom we give.

I love to give, but I hate to be taken. I'm very willing to be generous, but quickly bristle either if I feel I'm being taken advantage of (that turns me into a fool), or if I am not being appreciated.

Don't misunderstand. I don't need fawning appreciation. If I buy you a cup of coffee, don't send me flowers. But I have learned that too often I am over-reliant on the gratitude of others, and if I don't feel any kind of appreciation, then my joy in generosity evaporates. And when that happens, I am betting my joy on somebody else's response.

Miroslav Volf:

> *Recipients' ingratitude may be one of the most difficult obstacles for givers to overcome. Sometimes ... even a gift well given is received ungratefully.*
> *In* The Brothers Karamazov, *Fyodor Dostoyevsky recounted the meeting between the saintly Father Zosima and a 'lady of little faith'. She wanted to become a sister of mercy, and as she thought about it, she was*

*'full of strength to overcome all obstacles. No wounds,
no festering sores' could frighten her ... But what if the
patient didn't meet her with gratitude? she asked herself.
What if he began abusing and rudely commanding her,
'which often happens when people are in great suffering'?
Here is how she responded to her own question: 'I came
with horror to the conclusion that, if anything could
dissipate her love to humanity, it would be ingratitude.'*[11]

Barnabas' giving was not just an economic response
to a need, but an act of heart-felt worship. He gave
out to others, but he also gave up to God.

And as he freely gave, Barnabas was blessed. Perhaps, even
though he didn't give to be noticed, his generosity singled
him out, demonstrated his great character, and therefore
paved the way for his selection for greater things later.

That's right. Generosity was good for Barnabas.

# And when we give out and up like he did, it's good for us.

- - - - -

Recently a famous pastor's wife was captured on television
making a statement that really bristled the feathers of
some. Addressing their own congregation, and with her
husband smiling at her side, the lady concerned gave a
spontaneous and unguarded word of exhortation, which
went viral online in a thirty-six-second YouTube posting.
Her message was that when we obey God - and worship
Him - we are doing it for ourselves rather than for Him.

Around the world, there was lots of
growling. Condemnation was swift.

THERE ARE NO ORDINARY PEOPLE

The pastor's wife remained adamant in the face of huge criticism, saying that, while she could have articulated the concept better, she firmly believed that when we obey and worship God it does us good.

I admire the heart and the widely reputed kindness of this ministry couple. But, although, as the lady herself admits, her comments were clumsy, and could have given the impression that faith was little more than about self-improvement and having a greater sense of personal wellbeing, nevertheless, they contained a vital truth.

# Worship is good for us. Generosity is good for us.

A recent sociological survey featured in the book, *The Paradox of Generosity*, revealed that generosity is very good for us, and not in a silly, televangelist, 'Give and God will make you rich' way. Generosity not only blesses others, but brings a smile to our own hearts too.

> *First the more generous [we] are, the more happiness, health and purpose in life [we] enjoy. This association between generous practices and personal well-being is strong and highly consistent across a variety of types of generous practices and measures of well-being. Second, we have excellent reason to believe that generous practices actually create enhanced personal well-being. The association between generosity and well-being is not accidental, spurious, or simply an artifact of reverse causal influence.*[12]

The paradox is that in giving, we do get.

60

*People actually grow by giving themselves away.*
*By caring for other people, those who give generously*
*end up increasing the quality of their own lives.*[13]

And if generosity is good for us, the opposite is also true.

# Meanness will shrivel our souls.

-      -      -      -      -

There are a number of words used to describe the same condition.

Cheap. Tight. Skinflint. Stingy.

But my favourite is a word that isn't used quite so often these days.

Miserly.

Or miser.

Miser comes from the same root as another, more familiar, word.

Miserable.

Simply put, misers are miserable.

If in doubt, ask the classic cheapskate, Ebenezer Scrooge. Now that's a tight-fisted chap who didn't have to fend off too many party invitations (actually, he did refuse one, sneering at an opportunity to share in a yuletide feast with his nephew Fred).

The wizened creation of Charles Dickens, Scrooge epitomises meanness. Cold hearted and joyless, and the sworn enemy of festive fun in general and Christmas in particular, moneylender Scrooge is emotionally frigid.

And he is a serial taker. Dickens dubs him a 'squeezing, wrenching, grasping, scraping, clutching, covetous, old sinner'.[14]

His hapless clerk, Bob Cratchit, is forced to work grinding
hours for meagre pay, a 'mere fifteen bob', and he is unable to
afford a coat or provide his family with a Christmas meal.

But a series of vivid apparitions, the ghosts of Christmases
Past, Present and Yet to Come, shake the vinegary
Scrooge out of his grabbing, and he is a man reborn.

His bony fingers, seemingly locked for life
in a grasp, miraculously uncurl.

His chilly heart thaws, and then bursts with warmth.

The scowl is banished, sent packing by a broad, genuine smile.

The taker becomes a giver.

And Scrooge, who previously seemed to ration
his steps and his words, lest anything be wasted,
becomes a man giddy to change his world.

-     -     -     -     -

Being tight is hard work.

We've all been around people who work overtime to be last
in line when it comes to paying. At the coffee shop they
open the door and insist that you go in first. This is not out of
courtesy, but is a tactical manoeuvre ensuring that you get to
the counter before them, and will be more likely to flash your
credit card. Or at the end of a pleasant meal, their sudden
departure to the bathroom is timed precisely to coincide
with the arrival of the bill at the table. Returning from the
bathroom relieved, their relief is heightened by the knowledge
that you've paid in their absence. Irritating, especially when
some veneer their meanness by making a virtue of it, insisting
that they're thrifty, when in fact they're just squeakily tight.

Meanness leads to self-deception. We suffer from what Andy Stanley calls 'Affluenza'[15] – just as the person suffering from anorexia looks into the mirror but their debilitating illness doesn't allow them to see themselves as either thin or healthy, so our affluence means we don't see that we're rounded and thoroughly well-to-do. We all hear the statistics about wealth and poverty in the world, and how we're amongst the richest on the planet. But we just don't want to believe it. And so we play a little game of delayed conviction: just a little more, and then I'll be generous, which is a subtle form of rebellion. We don't outright refuse to be generous – we just delay it endlessly – so we might just as well refuse. Too many of us practise post-dated generosity: one day we'll get around to giving, but we mistakenly think that until we do, believing in the idea is enough. It isn't.

We're lulled into a life of grasping by a media that is fuelled by feeding our need for more. A US-based DIY chain tells us that we should never stop improving.

And we believe the spin.

Our appetite for stuff doesn't stay static, and invariably doesn't decrease, but expands – the more we have, the more we want.

We wrestle with a quiet fear that, like a man hanging on to a cliff ledge by his fingertips, if we loosen our grip, then we'll fall to our deaths.

We think the joy of giving, and the satisfaction that comes from knowing that we have brightened or even saved someone's life, is not as great as the joy that we'll get from stuff – and we believe a lie.

So let's demonstrate that we've uncovered the myth about grabbing.

# Let's choose to live generously, and not just with our stuff.

Give that stretch of tarmac to the bullish driver
who rudely cuts in during the rush hour.

Offer the rare gift of listening.

Instead of fuming over the man who stands in the 'five
items only' queue in the supermarket with eight items
in his basket, let's smile and wish him a pleasant day.

And if being miserly has made us miserable, let's not resign
ourselves to that pattern of living, or insist that we just
have to surrender to being the way we've always been.

We can change. We can become generous.
That's the gospel truth.

# Four:
## STAY HOME SOMETIMES

*'Then the high priest and all his associates, who were members of the party of the Sadducees, were filled with jealousy. They arrested the apostles and put them in the public jail. But during the night an angel of the Lord opened the doors of the jail and brought them out. "Go, stand in the temple courts," he said, "and tell the people all about this new life."' - Acts 5:17-20*

*'When the members of the Sanhedrin heard this, they were furious and gnashed their teeth at him. But Stephen, full of the Holy Spirit, looked up to heaven and saw the glory of God, and Jesus standing at the right hand of God. "Look," he said, "I see heaven open and the Son of Man standing at the right hand of God."*

*At this they covered their ears and, yelling at the top of their voices, they all rushed at him, dragged him out of the city and began to stone him. Meanwhile, the witnesses laid their coats at the feet of a young man named Saul.*

*While they were stoning him, Stephen prayed, "Lord Jesus, receive my spirit." Then he fell on his knees and cried out, "Lord, do not hold this sin against them." When he had said this, he fell asleep. And Saul approved of their killing him.*

*On that day a great persecution broke out against the church in Jerusalem, and all except the apostles were scattered throughout Judea and Samaria.' - Acts 7:54-8:1*

'I've never attended a "steadfast obedience"
party at work. I've never been invited to a
"staying put" get-together. I've never heard
of a "sticking around forever" shindig. And I
haven't for one simple reason: We live in a
corporate culture that celebrates people who
leave and ignores those who stay.' – Jon Acuff[1]

'The essential thing is ... long obedience in
the same direction' – Friedrich Nietzsche[2]

It is the sound of the blaring siren that
sends shivers down my spine.

The movie is *Schindler's List*, the harrowing epic based on
the life of Oskar Schindler, who did all he could to hide
Polish Jews from their Nazi hunters in the city of Krakow.

As a family scurries to their hiding place, they hear the
approaching siren of the SS truck. Their eyes widen with fear
as they realise that the siren is wailing in their street, and
then is outside the house where they have taken refuge.

Orders are barked in gruff, guttural tones, and there is the
ominous metallic sound of rifles hurriedly cocked.

Jackboots thud on the stairs. Furniture is overturned. And then,
the moment they've dreaded, as the hidden doorway to the
nook where they crouch is discovered. They are pinioned and
dragged downstairs, then hurled into the back of a truck and
taken to God only knows where. The hunters have their prey.

-      -      -      -      -

Luke uses a word in the Greek that suggests that the persecution in Jerusalem came like a sudden storm - which we have translated simply as 'great persecution broke out'.

Two heady years have passed since we last saw Barnabas. In that time, the church in Jerusalem had mushroomed; surprisingly, and controversially, a large number of Levites, like Barnabas, joined the ranks of the believers. The church was getting organised; deacons had been chosen to help with food distribution. But in a Jewish community huddled together for solace against the Roman occupiers, the threat that the Christians posed to national unity was never going to be tolerated.

And so the oppressed became the oppressors. The Jewish authorities turned on the Jesus followers. Initial persecution came to little, with the apostles summoned to two hearings before the Jewish hierarchy, the Sanhedrin. The first appearance resulted in a warning, but one that was muted because the Christians still had popular support. The community leaders were politically canny, and feared a riot if they handled the apostles too roughly.

The influence of the Christians widened, miracles happened but fear was beginning to surface too. The crowds wanted the power that the believers had, but they didn't want the pressure that they were living under, so were reluctant to join their ranks.

The apostles were arrested and thrown in jail, but there was an angelically assisted breakout (Acts 5:17-21).

They were arrested again, called to account for their actions, flogged and released, with yet more threats hanging over their heads. But they just kept doing what they were called to do: preaching, praying, healing, caring. They stuck at it.

Stephen, miracle worker and apologist, locked horns with a group from a local synagogue of Greek-speaking Zionists. He ended up before the same high council, preached an amazing sermon and paid for it with his life: they dragged him out and stoned him, laying their coats at the feet of a young zealot called Saul. Everything had changed for the Church, because the tide of popular opinion had turned against them. They were utterly vulnerable. And the young, zealous coat-keeper became an ethnic cleanser.

Acting like a wild animal hungry for blood, Saul began to destroy the Church. He made a house-to-house search for believers, not even sparing the women. Later, Saul was to write about his terrible campaign, his head and heart surely bowed in shame:

> I persecuted the followers of this Way to
> their death, arresting both men and women
> and throwing them into prison
>
> (Acts 22:4)

And again:

> On the authority of the chief priests I put many of
> the Lord's people in prison, and when they were
> put to death, I cast my vote against them. Many
> a time I went from one synagogue to another to
> have them punished, and I tried to force them to
> blaspheme. I was so obsessed with persecuting them
> that I even hunted them down in foreign cities.
>
> (Acts 26:10-11)

The believers that were especially targeted were the Greek-speaking Christian 'radicals', like Philip. The apostles and their fellow Aramaic-speaking Christians were not under such threat, because they continued in the Jewish traditions, and so, feeling a little more secure, they were able to stay in the city.

Many scattered, fleeing for safety – running from threat, but not running from their love for Jesus – those refugees shared the gospel far and wide as they went, ending up in Judea, Samaria, Phoenicia, Antioch of Syria and Cyprus.

Cyprus. Home to Barnabas, himself obviously a Greek-speaking Jew, and an ex-Levite to boot. A prime target. He could have fled from Jerusalem when the others did. But I believe that he stayed put.

-        -        -        -        -

Bear with me, because we need to do a little detective work. There's no biblical statement that specifically says that Barnabas stayed in Jerusalem during the terrible persecution spearheaded by Saul. But I believe that he did, and for good reason.

We're told that the apostles stayed. While Barnabas was not designated as an apostle at that point (that would come later),[3] Luke's wording doesn't deny that others stayed too; the Church continued to be headquartered in Jerusalem.

If Barnabas had gone with those who fled, there would have been no reason for him to have been sent later from Jerusalem to investigate the conversions that were happening in Antioch, because the 'scattered' were sharing Jesus in their new locations. He would have already been with those scattered, and would have returned to report, not been sent out to investigate.

And then Barnabas was on hand to be the 'bridge' person when Saul was converted and tried to join the Jerusalem church. Not only does that mean that Barnabas was obviously present and available at the time, but his opinion was valued and trusted: he had become a seasoned leader in the Church.

He could not know it, but Barnabas' decision to stay meant that when a delegate was needed for that delicate mission of investigating reports of Gentiles coming to faith, he was on hand and available to be sent.

# It's often said that our lives can turn on small hinge moments.

Those good choices that lead to opportunities that we never could have anticipated.

That shouldn't make us paranoid about our decision making, but should nudge us to make choices with careful, prayerful thought.

If I'm right, and Barnabas stayed put, his decision to remain in Jerusalem is not even mentioned. His courage carried no fanfare in the biblical record. But the vital principle is this: sometimes it takes more faith to stay than to go, and not just when a genocidal thug is knocking at your door.

-     -     -     -     -

Unsurprisingly, Christians are attracted to change, challenge and newness. Movement is in our blood. We're part of the Church, the *ekklesia*, the 'called-out' ones. Just as the Hebrews navigated the desert with God at their helm, a pillar of cloud by day, a pillar of fire by night, so we naturally see ourselves as people on the road. After all, Jesus called us to follow Him: that implies journey, mobility, steering through changing scenery. We're pioneers, we say, not settlers. Change is here to stay.

Some of us sniff haughtily at sameness. I've done it myself, foolishly mocking valuable traditions, practices well worth keeping because they've weathered the test of time, trashing them as traditionalism.

We rightly celebrate church planters, who relocate from where they are so that they can go to where God has called them to be. Missionaries, impossibly brave as they head towards uncertain horizons and unfamiliar cultures, are our heroes - and deservedly so.

Faith is getting out of the boat, we insist. Walking on the water. We don't so much worship change, but we're certainly enamoured with it.

But sometimes our thirst for the new and shiny is thinly disguised consumerism. A new church is launched in our town, and it quickly gains a reputation for being the next big thing. The worship is more exciting. The teaching is more illuminating and practical - or so they say. Soon a group of transient Christians show up, many of whom never stay in one church for too long. They left where they were, adamant that God told them to go, an insistence that's difficult to debate. Sadly, it won't be too long before He (apparently) gives them their marching orders again.

# Sometimes faith is not so much upping and leaving, but standing firm and staying.

There are some unsung heroes who do just that.

Digging in, they commit for the long haul.

Refusing to just engage in the popular habit of 'attending' church (you don't 'attend' a family), they graft themselves into the vision of that church: they work, they pray, they give, they endure.

When the local church is turbulent and seething with controversy, or when we discover people there that we just simply don't like, it's tempting to break camp, head somewhere else and enjoy the new-car-leather fragrance of another church. The grass is greener, and beckoning.

When a group of church planters are sent out, we gather around them and pray for grace for them as we go. But those who stay need grace too. There will be gaps to fill now. With those excited, edgy types gone, enthusiasm levels will be lower. The budget will be hit, their giving will be missed and those who stay will have to step up to the plate. Literally.

In Eugene Peterson's wonderful book *The Pastor*, he quotes Friedrich Nietzsche, the philosopher who was famous for his 'God is dead' pronouncements. Nietzsche coined the phrase, 'a long obedience in the same direction'. Peterson took that phrase seriously, and spent half a lifetime pastoring one church.

> *I was in the process of coming to terms with my congregation, just as they were: their less than developed emotional life, their lack of intellectual curiosity, the complacent acceptance of a world of consumption and diversion, their seemingly peripheral interest in God. I wasn't giving up on them. I didn't intend to leave them where I found them. By now I was prepared to enter a long process of growth in which they would discover for themselves the freshness of the Spirit giving vitality to the way they loved and worked and laughed and played. And I was finding areas of common ground that made us fellow pilgrims, comrades in arms in recognizing unexpected shards of beauty in worship and scripture and one another. I was learning not to impose my expectations of what I hoped for them, but rather let them reveal to me, as they were able, who they were. I was becoming a pastor who wasn't in a hurry.*[4]

Peterson stayed. And it's not just churches
that need people with faith to stay.

–     –     –     –     –

Richard Selzer, a surgeon as skilful with a pen as
he is with a scalpel, writes movingly in his epic
*Mortal Lessons: Notes on the Art of Surgery*:

> *I stand by the bed where a young woman lies, her face
> postoperative, her mouth twisted in palsy, clownish. A tiny
> twig of the facial nerve, the one to the muscles of her
> mouth, had been severed. She will be thus from now on.
> [I] had followed with religious fervor the curve of her flesh ...
> to remove the tumor in her cheek, I had cut the little nerve.*
>
> *Her young husband is in the room. He stands on the
> opposite side of the bed, and together they seem to dwell
> in the evening lamplight, isolated from me, private. Who
> are they, I ask myself, he and this wry-mouth I have made,
> who gaze at and touch each other so generously, greedily?*
>
> *The young woman speaks. 'Will my mouth always
> be like this?' she asks.*
>
> *'Yes,' I say, 'it will. It is because the nerve was cut.'
> She nods, and is silent. But the young man smiles.
> 'I like it,' he says, 'It is kind of cute.'*
>
> *All at once I know who he is. I understand, and I lower
> my gaze. One is not bold in an encounter with a god.
> Unmindful, he bends to kiss her crooked mouth, and I so
> close I can see how he twists his own lips to accommodate
> to hers, to show her that their kiss still works.*[5]

In the marriage ceremony, we pledge to stay. In sickness
and in health. When the bank balance is flush with surplus
funds, and when we fear our credit rating is seriously
unhealthy. We promise to turn our backs, our eyes,

our hearts away, forsaking all others, as long as we both shall live. Whatever might come, whatever allure might be shimmering before us, during the times when our love is more pedestrian than scintillating, we're going to stay.

In a culture where staying has become unfashionable, and where relationships are viewed by some as disposable, we have an epidemic of moving on - in all areas of life.

But it looks like Barnabas stayed. It wasn't exciting to do that. The knock on the door was never far away. If that's how it was, not only did he have grace to stay but, when the time finally did come for him to pack his bags, Barnabas was ready.

# He would have grace to go. And grace to stay.

# Five:
## BE VERY, VERY AFRAID

'Meanwhile, Saul was still breathing out murderous threats against the Lord's disciples. He went to the high priest and asked him for letters to the synagogues in Damascus, so that if he found any there who belonged to the Way, whether men or women, he might take them as prisoners to Jerusalem. As he neared Damascus on his journey, suddenly a light from heaven flashed around him. He fell to the ground and heard a voice say to him, "Saul, Saul, why do you persecute me?"

"Who are you, Lord?" Saul asked.

"I am Jesus, whom you are persecuting," he replied. "Now get up and go into the city, and you will be told what you must do."

The men travelling with Saul stood there speechless; they heard the sound but did not see anyone. Saul got up from the ground, but when he opened his eyes he could see nothing. So they led him by the hand into Damascus. For three days he was blind, and did not eat or drink anything.' – Acts 9:1-9

'When [Saul] came to Jerusalem, he tried to join the disciples, but they were all afraid of him, not believing that he really was a disciple.' – Acts 9:26

'why are you so afraid?' – Matthew 8:26

'Bran thought about it. "Can a man
still be brave if he's afraid?"
"That is the only time a man can be brave,"
his father told him.' - George R.R. Martin[1]

'I must say a word about fear. It is life's only
true opponent. Only fear can defeat life. It is
a clever, treacherous adversary, how well I
know. It has no decency, respects no law or
convention, shows no mercy. It goes for your
weakest spot, which it finds with unerring ease.
It begins in your mind, always ... So you must
fight hard to express it. You must fight hard
to shine the light of words upon it. Because
if you don't, if your fear becomes a wordless
darkness that you avoid, perhaps even manage
to forget, you open yourself to further attacks
of fear because you never truly fought the
opponent who defeated you.' - Yann Martel[2]

'I must not fear. Fear is the mind-killer. Fear is
the little-death that brings total obliteration.
I will face my fear. I will permit it to pass
over me and through me. And when it has
gone past I will turn the inner eye to see its
path. Where the fear has gone there will be
nothing. Only I will remain.' - Frank Herbert[3]

'Fear cuts deeper than swords.'
– George R.R. Martin[4]

'We fear being sued, finishing last, going
broke; we fear the mole on the back, the new
kid on the block, the sound of the clock as
it ticks closer to the grave.' – Max Lucado[5]

'I learned that courage was not the absence
of fear, but the triumph over it. The brave
man is not he who does not feel afraid, but he
who conquers that fear.' – Nelson Mandela[6]

At 1.20am, my mobile phone rang. Loudly. A shrill ringtone,
one that I selected in a moment of madness, pierced laser-
like through the thick layers of my deep sleep. I awoke
with a start, heart pounding, eyes suddenly wide. Within
a second, even before I had swung my feet out of the
bed, my mind had sprinted into adrenalin-laced action,
speculating wildly: whatever has happened? Most of my
friends don't phone me in the small hours for a happy little
chat, which is one reason why they're still my friends.

I couldn't find the phone, which continued shrieking
impatiently. In the darkness I bumped into a rather
solid piece of furniture, and uttered a word of praise
and thanksgiving (I wish) as I bruised myself.

As I stumbled frantically around the shadowy room at
534 mph, my mind was way ahead of me, travelling at
warp speed, hurtling through a horrifying catalogue of
possible reasons for the call. Someone in our family has

been in an accident/is terribly injured/is stranded in Latvia/ is lying cold in a mortuary, awaiting my identification. Fear creates endless chilling possibilities. At last I located the phone, and heard an unfamiliar voice ...

# But the voice that is all too familiar to most of us is the niggling whisper of fear.

We know it well. We're intimidated by its hiss.

Fear can speed through our minds at a rate faster than any Wi-Fi connection. Ignited and fuelled by imagination, fear is devastatingly effective at night; it mugs our exhausted minds and insists that we stay wide awake, restlessly fretting while the hands of the alarm clock crawl around the dial, silently tormenting us as we long for dawn to break. It punctuates our dreams with horror stories that drench us in cold sweat; we awake relieved, but hope it was just a dream and not a premonition.

\-         \-         \-         \-         \-

Fear.

It's probably the most effective weapon in the world today, quietly killing more people on the planet than even cancer. Its genius lies in the fact that, generally, it leaves little evidence that will be detected during a post-mortem. There's no exit wound, no bullet head, no gash where a knife penetrated skin. There will be organ damage in many cases, but although, for example, the heart gave up pumping earlier than anticipated, nobody will notice why.

Because of fear, nations will go to war, stock markets will tumble, businesses will collapse. Neighbours will despise the people next door, convinced that they are a menace.

Pinioned by fear, children will continue to allow their abusers to do their most terrible work, spouses will submit to another bruising beating. Because of fear, churches will gradually evolve into cults, with leaders who are Bible-carrying bullies calling the shots.

And the weapon of fear is so effective because, much of the time, it works with such subtlety. People will marry the wrong person because of it, terrified of being alone.

Fear demands that we shun golden opportunities, paralysed into inaction because of what might happen. And the weapon of fear has an ability to gnaw, to gently erode rather than instantly destroy: some will pay large sums for their dream holiday, but it will be a blighted paradise lost, the sunny days made cloudy, and all because, when they pack their bags, they take this cursed fear with them.

It's virulent too, like Ebola. The weapon is especially effective when unleashed in a group. Everyone within the group will be driven almost insane when infected by it and, desperate to escape its clutches, they'll do terrible things that, as thoughtful, generally good people, they'd never normally do.

# Fear. It's a weapon of mass destruction that is so very devastating.

We fear life. We fear death. We fear what is. We fear what is not, and we fear what might possibly be. Fear pushes us around, makes us freeze when we should flee, roughly shoves us into panic when calm reflection would be so much better. We're frightened of what we know, and terrified that there are awful factors behind everyday life that we don't know. It ruins our waking, and robs us of sleep. We're afraid of intimacy, rejection, heights and clowns. We fear failing, we fear spiders. I look into the eyes of my mother, broken as she is by dementia, and I hear fear's whisper: you're her son. You'll be just like her. I swat it away, but I know that I have only subdued it for now. It will be back.

Fear is fed by a media that knows that fear sells, so they'll traumatise us into buying. A survey of media by Frank Furedi showed that in 1994, the phrase 'at risk' occurred in UK newspapers 2,037 times. By the end of the next year the usage doubled, and, during 2000, the phrase was used 18,003 times.[7] Max Lucado responds to the bad news about bad news:

> Honestly, did world danger increase ninefold in six years? We are peppered with bad news. Global warming, asteroid attack, SARS, genocide, wars, earthquakes, tsunamis, AIDS ... Does it ever stop? The bad news is taking its toll. We are the most worried culture that has ever lived. For the first time since the end of the Second World War, parents expect that life for the next generation will be worse than it was for them.[8]

Sometimes politicians garner support by playing on, and even exploiting, our capacity to be afraid. During his presidential inauguration address of 1933, Franklin Roosevelt famously spoke of what people should really fear while facing the bleak reality of the Great Depression:

> So, first of all, let me assert my firm belief that the only thing we have to fear is fear itself - nameless, unreasoning, unjustified terror which paralyzes needed efforts to convert retreat into advance.[9]

Roosevelt's words are often attributed to Winston Churchill,
another politician who, instead of capitalising on fear,
led people forward into action despite their fears.

Clive Stafford Smith, writing in *Intelligent Life*
magazine, refers back to Roosevelt's speech:

> *The modern politician has forgotten Roosevelt's*
> *words. He [or she] prefers to play on fear – fear*
> *that prevents sensible action, and never inspires it.*
> *In America, many say we need the death penalty to*
> *prevent crime, thereby distracting us from demanding*
> *restrictions on guns, a wise drug policy, or adequate*
> *education. We are taught to fear terrorism to such an*
> *extent that we end up forfeiting our liberties, even if*
> *the chance of it affecting our lives is infinitesimal. We*
> *are told to fear losing our jobs to immigrants, rather*
> *than to the powerful who destroy the economy.*
>
> *Fear escalates in inverse proportion to experience.*
> *So white people in the white-flight suburbs of American*
> *cities fear crime far more than do black citizens in*
> *the city centres – because of, not despite, the fact that*
> *the suburban white is far less likely to be a victim.*
>
> *We spend hours catastrophising horrors*
> *that will never come to pass.*[10]

Fear strikes people of faith, and has been a curse since
the dawn of history, emptying Eden as Eve became
convinced by careless whispers that God surely couldn't
be trusted, and then passed on the virus to her man.

Fear paralysed Gideon, convinced as he was
that of all people, he was the least.

Elijah, rather famous for raising the dead, calling down fire from
heaven and an assortment of other miraculous happenings,
was finally taken out by a smart missile from Jezebel,

the Cruella de Vil of the Old Testament. Her explicit and violent threats turned the prophet into a terrified fugitive: after all that he accomplished, the Bible just records his terror:

*Elijah was afraid and ran for his life.*

(1 Kings 19:3)

When partying angels greeted bewildered shepherds near Bethlehem, their instruction was swift: 'Don't be afraid.' The same comforting command was issued to Mary, Elizabeth, Zechariah and Joseph. Fear threatened to neuter the good news that was being delivered to them.

# And fear almost meant that the Church lost Paul the apostle.

If fear had been allowed to run its course, the church at Jerusalem would have closed its heart to the former persecutor - with implications that are difficult to measure.

\-     \-     \-     \-     \-

Three more years or so had gone by. The Jerusalem church had regrouped, and, ironically, Saul's programme of persecution meant that the gospel was spreading far and wide. Instead of snuffing out the flame, it fanned it. Believers had gone down to Samaria, preaching as they went and then Philip, one of the scattered, had performed amazing miracles there. Such was the stir that the Jerusalem 'headquarters' sent Peter and John to investigate and be a part of it all. Philip continued his itinerant ministry, on the Gaza road and in towns and villages as far spread as Caesarea.

But faith today doesn't guarantee faith tomorrow. Back in Jerusalem, those who had once shown such courage gradually became fearful, their confidence eroded by time and weariness.

And so when Saul, the former architect of the great persecution, showed up, insisting that he had met Jesus, just about everyone was frozen with terror (Acts 9:26).

Someone had to bring a thaw to the freeze.

Barnabas again.

—     —     —     —     —

Was Barnabas afraid along with the rest of them? Some commentaries insist that he did not share their fear, but I can't see why. There's no reason to think he wasn't nervous. He had seen first-hand the carnage that Saul had masterminded. Having looked into the eyes of wives who'd lost husbands, taken away in the dead of night because of a knock on the door, he knew full well what this man was capable of. And Luke says that they were *all* afraid of Saul.

Fear is a complex issue, and one that won't be dealt with in a few sentences here – I wish! But as it relates to the story of Barnabas, what we see clearly is this: whether he felt the emotion of fear or not, the fact is that he refused to be controlled by it. And it's especially significant because a culture of fear was pervading the life of the apostles and the church there. It's one thing to wrestle with and conquer our own personal concerns privately, but when everyone around us is overcome with the same common fear, we reasonably assume that, because everyone is afraid, there must be very good reason to be terrified, and so we join in without hesitation.

# Barnabas did not succumb to that prevailing fog.

What he did do was to take action that was directly in rebellion to everything that fear might have dictated.

He could have been tempted to believe that everyone else was justified in their terror.

He could have stayed quiet.

In fact, he had a perfect excuse for silence.

At this time, it seems that he was not formally recognised as an apostle, and others in the room were. If anyone needed to break ranks, show true mettle as a leader and be brave, it should surely have been one of them. Barnabas might have reasoned like this: why would he want to contradict those dynamic leaders who had spent three years with Jesus? Keep quiet and be cautious, Barnabas. But he refused to give himself the excuse to play it safe.

And then, in taking Saul to the apostles, he led the man that everyone thought was a spy right into their inner circle of leadership. If Barnabas had been wrong, unparalleled disaster would have been the result. He might have rightly hesitated, congratulating himself that he'd been prudent, unwilling to put others at risk.

# Fear can present some rather convincing arguments for inaction.

Better to have been cautious.

No, he wouldn't be so headstrong, so arrogant.
Better to submit to their opinion.

Perhaps he took all of these possibilities into consideration, but then had such a clear sense that Saul was authentic, and therefore needed a warm welcome.

Barnabas stood at a junction: to allow fear to silence him, or allow faith to nudge him to step out, and call the others to join him in welcoming Saul. He chose the latter.

-       -       -       -       -

When it comes to fear, Jesus' teaching is stunningly blunt.

It's maddeningly simple with Him. He tells us this, when it comes to fear:

Don't.

What do You mean, Jesus, just 'don't'?

Does He know the world we live in?

'Don't be afraid,' He says (Matt. 10:31).

If I'm told not to do something, I must have the ability, with God's help, not to go there, to refuse fear's invitations. I'm wrong to cower powerless before the Goliath of fear. I might only have a makeshift catapult and a few stones in hand, but, by God (literally), I can topple that giant. And this is more than 'Don't worry, be happy'. I need to learn to replace my anxious thoughts with urgent volleys of prayer; according to Jesus, worry produces nothing, prayer changes everything (Luke 12:22–31, see also Phil. 4:6). I can place vivid imaginings of dread under arrest, taking my thoughts captive. Is it easy? No. Trust takes practice. Discipline. But just because it's easier said than done doesn't mean it can't be done.

Jesus is not calling us to ignore what might cause us to fear; on the contrary, He frequently warned people about difficult times ahead, perhaps to allow them to prepare emotionally, and know that, even in the most painful times, God was and is God.

And Jesus takes our capacity for fear seriously. Max Lucado notes that the most common command that Jesus gave shows that He knows how cowed we are before fear.[11] When asked what the most important commandment was, Jesus responded that it was to love God and love our neighbour, a command that's repeated eight times in the Gospels. But by far the most repeated command recorded by Jesus relates to fear. No fewer than twenty-one times, Jesus calls us either not to be afraid, to take heart or to be of good cheer.

And He's surely not calling us to pretend that we'll never be touched emotionally by fear.

But there's a huge difference between feeling afraid and being paralysed by fear.

# Fear may touch us, but we don't have to allow it to grasp us, to arrest us.

Recognise the fear, but don't allow it to manacle your feet.

That's what Jesus did with His own fear. Gethsemane was a place of abject terror. The temptation was surely this: run for Your life, literally. But He allowed Himself to be arrested. He wouldn't allow what He felt to derail Him.

That took effort. Wrestling, sweating what seemed like great drops of blood.

He worked at praying instead of fretting.

# Fear won't be tackled by idleness.

It will take a battle to arrest those tormenting thoughts and realise that, much of the time, fear threatens

us with possibilities that never become realities,
as my nocturnal phone caller taught me.

It turns out that an airline that had damaged a bag during a
recent trip decided to return it in the middle of the night. A nice
delivery chap explained to me that he had my bag and was
just ten minutes away. Stifling a scream, I gently advised him
that it was the middle of the night. It's an empty bag, I told him,
for which I have no immediate need. But he was determined.

He called me three more times for directions.

Finally, at 2am he arrived. I had a blissful reunion with my
bag, and treated it like a returning prodigal, I'd missed it
so. I thanked him warmly - he was just doing his job.

And as I wandered back to bed, I realised that my fears, so vivid
and terrifying just a minute or two ago, were quite groundless.

They usually are.

Let's take Roosevelt's advice.

Be very, very afraid.

Of fear itself.

But then allow Jesus, who commands us not to
be afraid, to teach us how to do just that.

Refuse fear.

# Six:
## GENERALLY, BELIEVE THE BEST

*'When he came to Jerusalem, he tried to join the disciples, but they were all afraid of him, not believing that he really was a disciple. But Barnabas took him and brought him to the apostles.' – Acts 9:26-27*

*'Then after three years, I went up to Jerusalem to get acquainted with Cephas and stayed with him fifteen days. I saw none of the other apostles – only James, the Lord's brother.' – Galatians 1:18-19*

'Love chooses to believe the best about people. It gives them the benefit of the doubt. It refuses to fill in the unknowns with negative assumptions. And when our worst hopes are proven to be true, love makes every effort to deal with them and move forward. As much as possible, love focuses on the positive.' – Stephen and Alex Kendrick[1]

'I always prefer to believe the best of everybody; it saves so much trouble.' – Rudyard Kipling[2]

'I still believe, in spite of everything, that people are truly good at heart.' – Anne Frank[3]

The Jews have a saying: 'If not for that day.'

They're referring to turning point days in our lives, when, quite simply, everything changes. We didn't know it when we swung our legs out of bed that morning. No email appeared, no phone rang to warn us: this is one of your biggest days on earth.

This is the day when: you'll find faith, meet your life partner, see a career door open or get that opportunity to emigrate.

Such days are turnstile days.

As we go through them, it is not that one aspect of our lives is different: everything, affecting our families, relationships, career, church, community, moves into a different gear.
We go through the turnstile as one person, and emerge another.

# Sometimes the turnstile is excruciatingly painful.

An accident, a virus, a call from the doctor's office about us or from the hospital about someone we love. A letter from the bank announcing that our mortgage is being cancelled. A redundancy notice. But, positively or negatively, we know that, because of that day, we are never, ever going to be the same again.

-       -       -       -       -

That night, I thought they'd mistaken me for someone else.

I've written about it elsewhere, and referred to that wonderful evening in countless sermons, so I'll keep it brief. I didn't come from a Christian home. A few trips to Sunday School had not been impressive, either for me, or for the long-suffering ladies who tried to teach me with their flannelboard. I thought all Christians needed treatment for mental health issues, and so had less than zero interest in getting any kind of religion.

I didn't realise that the evening service would include baptisms in water, by full immersion. That meant that I witnessed what appeared to be an aquatic mugging, as each of those being baptised briefly told their stories, and then went down into the tank and got very, very wet.

I was impressed and confused in turn, and decided to let confusion win, and fled the place. Sitting outside in my car, I lit a cigarette and, swearing profusely, I vowed to my friend Ian that I'd never darken the doors of a church again. Then I realised that I'd left my coat in the church building.

I only went back for my coat.

Can I have my coat, please?

What I got was a new life.

A chap approached me. Malcolm, one of those who had been baptised.

'Hello. Are you a Christian?' he asked, no hint of aggression or interrogation, a warm smile on his face.

'Of course I am,' said I. 'I'm British.'

Suddenly I knew that I was not anything of the sort, and, for no reason that I can explain, I wanted to be. So did Ian. 'What do we need to do?' we asked.

The now broadly grinning chap advised us that we would need to go to the little room at the back, where we'd be told what Christian commitment would mean.

We both said yes.

Yes to going to the little room at the back, which was somewhat scary.

Yes to Jesus, who was less so.

We knelt on the floor, and prayed our prayers of commitment.

And then we opened the door of that little room, expecting to find an empty building.

But word had got around. There are pagans in the house, and they are getting converted.

More than excitement was in the air – there was genuine welcome, because a long greeting line snaked to the back of the building. Ian and I had to go down that line, receiving handshakes and hugs. I met Kay, my wife-to-be, in that line (although she had her eye on Ian ...).

We were teenagers, Ian and I. I had long hair. Beads. I had been the first one to get drunk at every party. We'd planned a boys' holiday with a group of pals that, suffice it to say, was about becoming fully 'adult' in our behaviour. We didn't look like potential givers, potential leaders, potential anything. But we got a royal welcome. I couldn't get over it then, and still haven't.

I was home.

But it doesn't always happen that way.

-        -        -        -        -

His name was Saul. As we've seen, he'd been a fanatical persecutor of the Church. But all of that had changed.

Three years earlier he'd been converted, but not through any witness or outreach of a church, which probably complicated things for him, because there were no trusted witnesses to his turning. His conversion had been dramatic. Blind for three days without food and drink, he'd then been baptised.

He soon began preaching in the synagogues of
Damascus, but came up against some zealous
Jews, and had to be smuggled out of town.

Then, a season in Arabia, and back to
Damascus once again (Gal. 1:17).

But incredibly, Saul waited for three years
before making the trek to Jerusalem.

Perhaps he hesitated because of his history there. The last time
he had been there he had rampaged through the city, dragging
believers out of their homes and putting them in prison. Now
he would be returning as a follower of the same Way he had
once tried to destroy. But surely, he might have mused, there
would be celebration and welcome. The persecuting prodigal
had come home. He'd proved his commitment: baptised, a
preacher, persecuted, he'd even survived an assassination plot.

He'd been welcomed and helped by the Christians in
Damascus, who had saved his life when they smuggled him out
of town (Acts 9:25). Surely he'd find an open door in Jerusalem?

Or maybe not.

—      —      —      —      —

You can't blame them really. The Christian community in
Jerusalem would surely have heard of Saul's conversion,
but may have scoffed at the reports, seeing this as just
another ploy of the arch-enemy of the Church to infiltrate
their ranks as a spy, and then wreak more havoc.

And so, when he tried to join them, Saul was offered a
very cold shoulder: in fact they froze him out. As we might
expect from Saul, he kept trying, despite their rebuffs. The
language that Luke uses speaks of repetitive persistence.

And then came a moment upon which history hinged. Barnabas consistently proved to be one who gave the benefit of the doubt and so, naturally, it was his instinct to do that here.

Whether it was a spontaneous or pre-meditated act, Barnabas stepped forward, hand extended. I love the way Luke describes the intervention by simply saying, 'But Barnabas' (Acts 9:27).

Sometimes all it takes is for one person to step out of line, and open their heart.

'But Barnabas.'

It's a graphic picture, not just of a handshake of welcome, but of Barnabas taking Saul by the hand and presenting him to the apostles. In standing with him, standing alongside him, Barnabas was saying to the Jerusalem leadership: you accepted and welcomed me, so now do the same with him.

His heart was probably in his mouth as he did it. John Sloan, a literary editor and author, paints a vivid picture of the tension that Barnabas must have felt:

> What Barnabas did was not easy. Imagine this assignment. It's 1960 in the American South. A man who waged a homicidal drive to inflict pain on you and your friends because of your commitment to racial equality has just dropped by your house to tell you he's had a change of heart. Not knowing whether to answer the door with a weapon in hand – since his hobbies have included cross burnings and late-night beatings – you crack the door just enough to see that he is unarmed. He says he really does want to make it right with you and those who have suffered because of his hatred. But he needs your help. You have heard that his violent crusade of hate has lost momentum and that his racist organization has fallen apart. You and your friends have thought that maybe he had a mental

*collapse. He had been a hatemonger. Now he is just a loser.*
*And since the tide of public sentiment is finally turning in*
*favor of civil rights, you can just turn the other direction and*
*pretend the guy doesn't exist. But he has become a Christian,*
*he says. What will it mean if you accept this man's story?*
*It will involve going to meetings with him where you will*
*encounter fathers who have lost sons to his persecutions,*
*mothers whose daughters have been abused because of his*
*hate, humble people who just wanted to live like everyone*
*else who walks up on the earth but were denied that right*
*because of the prejudice of people like this man. You will*
*have to face groups who adamantly believe the guy is not*
*worth saving. 'My daughter will never get a second chance,'*
*one woman in your group will say. 'This man caused so*
*much heartache that we'll never be able to forgive him,'*
*another will shout. And in many ways you'll hear yourself*
*agreeing with them. He doesn't deserve a second chance.*
*Would you stand up for this guy? Barnabas wouldn't hesitate.*[4]

I don't think Barnabas had any inkling that this man he
welcomed would someday write thirteen books of the
New Testament. Barnabas would never know what a New
Testament is. And he surely had no clue that Saul would
become Paul, and preach the gospel from Jerusalem to Rome.

# Let's take risks for love. Bet on the losers, knowing that sometimes they might just win and prove everyone wrong.

Let's be extraordinary people as we break ranks with those who
love to carp and gossip, especially when they're whispering about
those we love. Let's interrupt, cut across the viral conversations
and defend those who are not there to defend themselves.

If it's in our power to do so, let's give people who think they have a gift a chance to prove it, develop it, grow in it.

Let's take responsibility for welcome, and not excuse ourselves by saying that it's somebody else's job.

When others insist that past performance speaks of what will happen in the future, let's give the offender a break, another chance, another shot at goal.

Let's risk guilt by association because we hang out with the wrong kind of people.

And when someone proves to be persistently 'difficult', let's go the extra mile with them: perhaps, in the final few hundred metres, they'll change their tune.

Let's not live our lives suspiciously, hurrying to judge a book by its cover and being delighted when we're proved to be right in our suspicions.

Let's be brave, and break step with popular opinion. Crowds can be wrong; if we're humbly, thoughtfully and prayerfully convinced that the current 'group think' is wrong, let's be bold enough to speak up - and humble enough to be quiet if we're proven correct.

In short, let's believe the best.

Generally.

-    -    -    -    -

If you're sensing a hesitation, you'd be quite right. Why am I qualifying this encouragement to believe the best with the word generally?

It's simple.

Sometimes believing the best is precisely
the opposite of what we should do.

Abusers have infiltrated churches and groomed children for
their terrible schemes, and, when suspicions were aroused,
nobody took action, because they wanted to believe the best.

Wives have been battered by brutes called husbands, but they
weren't believed, because nobody wanted to believe the worst.

Smooth operators have developed Ponzi schemes and targeted
Christians, playing the card of their feigned integrity.

And so, sometimes, not only do we need to be willing
to believe the worst, but we must give permission to
others to believe the very worst of us, allowing them
to challenge our behaviour, without responding with
a rebuff of 'How could you think such a thing?'

Barnabas deserves our congratulation and appreciation
because, in his brave, risky act, he has shown us
how to step out and step up with love. And he didn't
always enjoy appreciation for what he'd done, even
from the one for whom he took such risks.

That might include Saul.

-        -        -        -        -

Later, Saul, having had a name change, would write
about that fateful fifteen-day visit to Jerusalem, when
he finally got acquainted with the church there.

Telling his friends in the Galatian churches the story of that trip,
he would mention meeting Peter, and James as well (Gal. 1:18-19).

In other words, Paul was quick to mention
the 'famous names' of Jerusalem.

THERE ARE NO ORDINARY PEOPLE

But there's no mention at all of Barnabas'
vital role in brokering that meeting.

And it would have been natural for Paul to mention Barnabas'
role, because Barnabas played such a part in helping plant
the churches of Galatia. As it turns out, while there is one
general reference to Barnabas in Galatians, the other is
extremely critical of him. As we'll see, these two men were
to fall out at least twice – once over eating habits, and then
over personnel. Some say that, when Paul wrote Galatians,
he was estranged from Barnabas; their relationship was
difficult, and after a brief reconciliation, it shattered again.[5]

Whatever the reason, when Paul wrote about
the fateful Jerusalem meeting, Barnabas was not
credited by Paul for his risky intervention.

And that's the way it often is.

Our risks for love, our refusal to traffic rumours, our
intervention to prevent gossip spreading, our insistence on
loyalty, sometimes go unheralded, uncelebrated, unnoticed.

But the fruit is certainly noticed, ultimately. What
might have become of the Church if we had lost
Saul/Paul because of fear and suspicion?

'But Barnabas.'

Thank God he broke ranks.

# Seven:
## FOR GOD'S SAKE, LISTEN

*'But Barnabas took [Saul] and brought him to the apostles. He told them how Saul on his journey had seen the Lord and that the Lord had spoken to him, and how in Damascus he had preached fearlessly in the name of Jesus. So Saul stayed with them and moved about freely in Jerusalem, speaking boldly in the name of the Lord.' – Acts 9:27-28*

'Listen to the conversations of our world, between nations as well as those between couples. They are for the most part dialogues of the deaf.' – Dr Paul Tournier[1]

'When people talk, listen completely. Most people never listen.' – Ernest Hemingway[2]

'You cannot truly listen to anyone and do anything else at the same time.' – M. Scott Peck[3]

'Listening is a magnetic and strange thing, a creative force. The friends who listen to us are the ones we move toward. When we are listened to, it creates us, makes us unfold and expand.' – Karl A. Menninger[4]

'Attention is the rarest and purest form of generosity.' – Simone Weil[5]

'Let a fool hold his tongue and he will pass for a sage.' – Publilius Syrus[6]

He always refused to eat baked potatoes, said he hated the 'jackets', potatoes with the skin left on.

I never understood why, having never come across potato prejudice before.

He was my father, and he spent four years of his youth in prison.

Captured during the Second World War in the North African desert, he spent those years incarcerated in Italian and German prison camps, until, finally, he escaped.

He was from a generation that, in looking back, didn't talk much about their suffering.

And sadly, I didn't ask too many questions. I know that those years were excruciatingly painful, and fuelled a dangerous, irrational prejudice. Long after the war was over, he harboured a simmering hatred for Italians. On a number of occasions, my mother had to steer him away from randomly punching any chap who was unfortunate enough to look remotely Mediterranean.

A whole decade after my father passed away, I discovered two documents buried at the bottom of an old file of his. One was a telegram informing my grandparents that my father was missing, presumed dead. They spent six harrowing months wondering if their only son had perished. And then there was a second telegram, this one from the Red Cross, telling them that he had survived but was being held in a German stalag, which was just a few miles from Auschwitz.

Prior to the internet, I would have had to criss-cross Europe and scour endless libraries in order to fill in the many blanks about those lost years of his. But now, armed with a date and a stalag number, I typed the details into a search bar, and in seconds my father's world of seventy-five years ago flashed instantly onto the screen.

I saw grainy, black and white photographs of men manacled by the neck, chained like animals. I read reports of 'slackers' being shot in the back of the head because they weren't working hard enough. I read about the death march that he was taken on, in the coldest winter of a hundred years. Men staggered along frozen roads for weeks, almost starving, eventually not even stopping to relieve themselves – just soiling themselves as they shuffled on, broken and exhausted. Those who fell were dispatched by a rifle butt to the neck.

He escaped from that march, and made his way to the house of a German family, where he asked for a meal, including potatoes. Peeled potatoes.

And an internet search showed me one more insight into his behaviour.

Every day, back in the prisoner-of-war camp, their rations were meagre. Nothing for breakfast.

Watery soup with a tiny square of often mouldy bread at lunchtime.

In the evenings, two or three potatoes, usually rotten.

And those potatoes were always doled out with their skins, their jackets on.

That's why he hated them so. For all those years, I never knew, and it was not just because he was so private.

I never asked. He lost much of his youth, and almost died, but I didn't make the effort to inquire, or take the time to listen.

He told me a little about those terrible years, but I never used the phrase, which, according to Dary Northrop (Senior Pastor of Timberline Church), is so vital in our relationships:

'Tell me more.'

In the age of the 'selfie', people who show authentic interest in anything other than themselves are increasingly rare.

It's a good thing that there was one member of the church in Jerusalem who was wasn't just preoccupied with self-preservation.

History would have taken a very different course.

-     -     -     -     -

We've already seen that Barnabas stepped up and intervened to break the freeze of fear that was preventing Saul from getting a welcome in the Jerusalem church.

# But Barnabas did more than insist that Saul be received and trusted.

Some translations describe this episode with the phrase, 'Barnabas helped Saul'. And that help came because Barnabas was able to recount Saul's story in careful detail, like a witness in a courtroom. He did it in a way that totally convinced the terrified apostles to change their stance from hostile rejection to a warm embrace.

For Barnabas to be able to tell Saul's story, he had to have
listened to it in the first place. He had given Saul a careful
hearing before he could then represent him fully at what might
have felt like a court hearing instead of a church gathering.

When people tell us about terrible difficulties that
they're walking through, we can feel helpless, and even
apologise because we sense we have little to say that is
helpful - as if the only time we're being useful is when
we're doing the speaking. But often we are the most help
not as we speak, but just as we listen. In fact, often we
dilute our helpfulness by breaking our silent listening too
soon, and in haste proffer a slogan or cliché in a clumsy
attempt at trying to offer a solution or an explanation.

Luke gives us details of how Barnabas knew and told Saul's
story. He's not content to record that Barnabas 'vouched' for
the former killer. The word Luke uses means that Barnabas
'declared fully, in detail' Saul's journey into faith. The Greek
word is similar to our word 'digest'. Careful hearing meant that
Barnabas had ruminated and pondered Saul's biography.

He knew Saul's conversion story - what happened, and
where it happened. He'd seen the Lord, and that epic
encounter took place on the road to Damascus.

Barnabas reported what Jesus had done
during that event; He spoke to Saul.

He told them what had been happening in Saul's life since
that junction moment. He'd been preaching in Damascus.

And he concluded by letting the fearful apostles
know that Saul had already paid a very high price
for his faith. He had been preaching boldly.

Barnabas was looking for far more than
a basic welcome for Saul.

# He was seeking apostolic endorsement for him.

That's why he took Saul to the apostles, and not just to the wider congregation. And that's why the detail that Saul had 'seen the Lord' was included in Barnabas' testimony: seeing the Lord was, at that time, a prerequisite for being an apostle.

Ever generous, once again Barnabas shows us that generosity is not just about stuff, or even giving the priceless gift of trust. The gift of hearing another person, and not just listening mechanically by offering silence, but listening with the heart, giving our full attention, is one of the most magnificent and valuable gifts we can offer. Rachel Naomi Remen puts it like this:

> The most basic and powerful way to connect to another person is to listen. Just listen. Perhaps the most important thing we ever give each other is our attention.[7]

Barnabas spoke, and told the story. The church apostles heard, and Saul's ministry was freely released and recognised. But, before any of that could have happened, Barnabas had to have listened carefully first.

Listening.

It's not so hard.

But it is so very rare.

- - - - -

It's a little game that Kay and I have played over the years of our travels. We've probably covered three million miles in ministry, and met countless people in our trekking.

The rules of the game are simple: when we fly in for ministry and are met at an airport, or connect with a leader for the first time over a meal or before a church service, we're fascinated to see how much interest, if any, they actually show in us.

We're normally asked how our flight went, where we've come in from, even what the food was like while we were airborne.

But then the interest generally tapers off quickly, and conversation switches to their life, their church, their concerns. I'm not bleating here, just stating a sad fact.

People who show any kind of deeper interest or genuine concern are extremely rare. But when we meet someone who *is* interested, it's like sunshine breaking out behind the clouds on an otherwise gloomy day.

And that's not surprising.

# When we're listened to, we're quietly discovering care, interest and significance.

This person's attentiveness shows that they want me, and not just what I can bring. They respect me enough to ask my opinion, and give me space to express it. My contribution is valued. I matter to them. I feel even more special if, when they speak, they address me by name.

People pay large sums of money to trained professionals who, among other things, give them a safe, predictable space where they will be heard.

And when there is an absence of listening, there is hurt. Michael P. Nichols explains:

> *Nothing hurts more than the sense that people close*
> *to us aren't really listening to what we have to say.*
> *We never outgrow the need to communicate what*

*it feels like to live in our separate, private worlds of experience. That's why a sympathetic ear is such a powerful force in human relationships – and why the failure to be heard and understood is so painful.*[8]

Churches are discovering the value of not just speaking at people, but listening to them.

Young church planters in Japan are experimenting with 'listening shops': tables in the local shopping centre with a sign that simply says, 'We listen'.

Takeshi Takazawa describes what happens:

*You sit in the middle of the city with a sign ... A lot of people stop and want to talk to you ... not a lot of explanation ... people feel it or experience it ... You just listen to the people ... As you listen their heart is opened up and usually they ask you why are you doing this, or what happened to you ... Then that's the opening of sharing your life ... not some idea or philosophy or logic ... your story merges with the other person's story.*[9]

In a world of apparent connection through social networking, where we can all broadcast the tiniest details of our lives in a few seconds, there's a famine of real listening. We're all busier than ever. I'm often saddened to walk into a restaurant and see people out for dinner together but glued to their smartphones, texting and updating their social media accounts, apparently more interested in people other than those they're sharing a table with.

And then, although it pains me to say it, I wonder how many people are actually really interested in others – and this includes those in the church community. In a world of soundbites, where our distractions are high and our boredom threshold low, we can end up with lots of acquaintances where superficial communication is the norm, but with few friends who really care for us or know us. And this can happen with people that we really love, as we unwittingly listen to something they're sharing for a few minutes, but then turn the conversation back around to our thoughts, our concerns, our story. Tournier is right. There are too many dialogues of the deaf.

There's a risk that we personally rush to conclude that we are rather good listeners. We assume that, because listening is a basic part of everyday life, we are accomplished at it.

# We may be thinking that we are better listeners than we actually are.

Perhaps we should ask our closest, trusted family members and friends to tell us how they rate us as listeners. And it goes without saying that we need to listen carefully to their response.

Let's listen. For God's sake.

And, if we do, we'll truly be rare, extraordinary human beings.

# Eight:
## UNDERGO OPEN-HEART SURGERY

*'Now those who had been scattered by the persecution that broke out when Stephen was killed travelled as far as Phoenicia, Cyprus and Antioch, spreading the word only among Jews. Some of them, however, men from Cyprus and Cyrene, went to Antioch and began to speak to Greeks also, telling them the good news about the Lord Jesus. The Lord's hand was with them, and a great number of people believed and turned to the Lord.*

*News of this reached the church in Jerusalem, and they sent Barnabas to Antioch. When he arrived and saw what the grace of God had done, he was glad and encouraged them all to remain true to the Lord with all their hearts. He was a good man, full of the Holy Spirit and faith, and a great number of people were brought to the Lord.' – Acts 11:19–24*

*'For the LORD is good and his love endures for ever; his faithfulness continues through all generations.' – Psalm 100:5*

'There is no greatness where there is not simplicity, goodness and truth.' – Leo Tolstoy[1]

'In Christ we see a maturity of love that flowers in self-sacrifice and forgiveness;

a maturity of power that never swerves
from the ideal of service; a maturity of
goodness that overcomes every temptation,
and, of course, we see the ultimate victory
of life over death itself.' – Vincent Nichols[2]

'Goodness is the only investment that
never fails.' – Henry David Thoreau[3]

'Barnabas clearly and consistently recognised
God's grace in unlikely people – the
murderer Saul, the uncircumcised gentiles
in Antioch, and his cousin John Mark who
seemed a fearful, spineless deserter, an early
casualty on the mission field. He sought
them out.' – Robin Gallaher Branch[4]

He was heralded simply as 'a good man'.

His was the most delicate of missions. Nothing less than the
future stability of the entire world hung upon it. As a diplomat,
he would endure hollow promises, staged false announcements
and hysterical screaming and bluster. When he returned
back to home base with a positive report, everyone breathed
a sigh of relief. But, tragically, he misread the situation.

He was Neville Chamberlain, the Prime Minister of Britain in
turbulent 1938. Germany was annexing parts of Czechoslovakia,
and Chamberlain naively believed that Adolf Hitler merely
wanted rights for German citizens living in the borderlands;
he didn't suspect that Hitler had much wider ambitions.

With a threat of war rumbling, Chamberlain arrived in Cologne on 22 September 1938, was welcomed with flowers and serenaded by a German band playing *God Save the King*. As negotiations continued through the ensuing week, in a mood of buoyant optimism President Franklin Roosevelt telegraphed Chamberlain with the words, 'Good man'. On 30 September 1938, Hitler, Chamberlain and other key European leaders signed the Munich Agreement. Later that day, after some rest, Chamberlain went to Hitler and asked him to sign a peace treaty between the United Kingdom and Germany, and Hitler happily agreed. But all was not as it seemed.

Upon his return to Britain, Chamberlain delivered his infamous 'Peace for our time' speech to crowds in London. The streets were so packed with cheering people it took Chamberlain an hour and a half to journey the nine miles from Heston to Buckingham Palace, where he was greeted as a hero by the royal family and invited onto the balcony at Buckingham Palace. But in Parliament there was opposition from the start from key players, including Winston Churchill, who grumbling but prophetically announced, 'England has been offered a choice between war and shame. She has chosen shame and will get war.'[5]

Back in Germany, Hitler regarded Chamberlain with utter contempt, specifically as 'an impertinent busybody who spoke the ridiculous jargon of an outmoded democracy'.[6] Hitler continued his aggression by invading Poland, Britain declared war on Germany on 3 September 1939, and Chamberlain led Britain through the first eight months of the Second World War before resigning in 1940, and dying six months later from cancer. The good man who had longed for peace died in the midst of war, all of his diplomatic efforts having come to nothing, shredded by Hitler.

Thousands of years earlier, another delicate diplomatic mission was launched.

Make no mistake.

This was no mere ecclesiastical investigation, as the church in Jerusalem heard of many Gentiles coming to faith in Antioch. If they had sent the wrong person to investigate what was going on, there could have been a massive division in the Church, with unthinkable ramifications for the unfolding history of the world.

A canny, open-minded, discerning diplomat was needed. A good man.

\-     \-     \-     \-     \-

Eight or nine years had passed; tumultuous years. Saul had suffered another death threat, this time in Jerusalem, from the old rivals of the Church - the Hellenistic Jews. Just as he'd escaped from Damascus, lowered in a basket from the city wall there, he had to get out of the city of Jerusalem quickly, not least because Jesus told him to. Years later Paul would reflect on the experience:

> When I returned to Jerusalem and was praying at the temple, I fell into a trance and saw the Lord speaking to me. 'Quick!' he said. 'Leave Jerusalem immediately, because the people here will not accept your testimony about me.'
>
> 'Lord,' I replied, 'these people know that I went from one synagogue to another to imprison and beat those who believe in you. And when the blood of your martyr Stephen was shed, I stood there giving my approval and guarding the clothes of those who were killing him.'
>
> Then the Lord said to me, 'Go; I will send you far away to the Gentiles.'
>
> (Acts 22:17-21)

As Paul exited the scene for some years and headed for his home town of Tarsus (nothing is known about his time there), the Church enjoyed a season of peace and consolidation. During this time, a church in Galilee was mentioned for the first time (Acts 9:31).

Peter's ministry continued, but was moving into an entirely new phase. The gospel was about to explode in the Gentile world, with the conversion of Cornelius, a Roman centurion. This was a cataclysmic development for the Church, so much so that Peter had to experience a waking vision containing direct instructions from the Lord before his brain and heart could countenance such a groundbreaking event (Acts 10). And the Holy Spirit took the initiative – while Peter was talking with Cornelius and his Gentile friends and family, the Spirit came upon them all, to the astonishment of the Jewish Christians who were part of Peter's group. Word got out, and Peter initially faced strong criticism but, after reporting all that God had done, the Jerusalem church celebrated that the gospel was being made available even to the Gentiles (a rather overdue realisation and celebration, because years earlier Jesus had told them to go into all the world. Sometimes we're slow to get it ...).

And so, at last, the gates of the Church were swinging wide open. And the first major influx of Gentile converts was about to arrive: the Church, at last, was moving into its worldwide mission, with all of the tensions and questions that this move would generate. But that ingathering didn't begin in Jerusalem, even though the city and the church there had been the centre of everything up until that point.

# The Jerusalem leaders had already been forced to adjust their thinking about apostleship.

Saul had been called by God completely independently of their sanction or approval. And the next great step forward for the Christian Church was to come, not as a result of a decision made in Jerusalem, but as a result of the evangelistic zeal of those refugees who were scattered by persecution years earlier. They hadn't even been formally sent out on mission; they had just fled, and lived as missionaries as they went. Because of their efforts, and the help of the Holy Spirit, another church in another city had been birthed. Luke now swings his literary camera around, away from Jerusalem, and focuses on that other city.

Antioch.

-     -     -     -     -

It was the New York of the day. A thriving cosmopolitan port town, renowned for its beauty (it was known as the 'Golden City'), Antioch boasted a high street that was four miles long and paved with marble. The third largest city in the Roman Empire, it teemed with half a million people. But not everything was beautiful.

Pagan worship was rife: a goddess called Daphne was worshipped there. Five miles outside the city, in a laurel grove, stood the temple dedicated to her worship. But what happened within those walls was a vile distortion of worship, as temple prostitutes gave themselves to countless men in bizarre and perverse 'rituals'.

Throughout the ancient world, the term 'the morals of Daphne' was used to describe depravity: the city was infamous.

And suddenly, within this messy place,
Gentiles were turning to Jesus.

Awkward.

# The Jerusalem church had a problem.

It was one thing to see Gentiles coming to faith in Christ – that was shocking enough – but what steps would they need to take once they were part of the Christian family? This was a theological and social earthquake. The Early Church constantly battled with those who insisted that following Christ meant adopting circumcision and other Jewish rituals. We'll look later at some of the conversations and even battles that took place around this teaching. But at this stage in the Early Church's history, those conversations had not been had, and so the issue had not been aired or settled.

The leaders in Jerusalem needed to send someone to Antioch, someone they trusted implicitly, who would tread carefully, investigate what was happening prayerfully and exercise discernment and wisdom. Once again, the stakes were high.

What was needed was not a few good men, but a really good man, to visit the fledgling church at Antioch and then report back.

The decision was made. A 'good man' was appointed to the task.

Barnabas. A good man.

Only one other person is described as 'good' in the book of Acts.

Perhaps truly good people are rare. And often uncelebrated.

-      -      -      -      -

# Goodness is a word in need of rehabilitation.

These days, it's not cool to be good, although that's no new phenomena. William Wilberforce, famous for his anti-slavery campaigning, also sought to 'make goodness fashionable'[7] in the culture of his day. We could use his influence and voice today.

Actress Keira Knightley recently admitted she was a 'boring' teenager. The film star 'confessed' she had never skipped school. Keira said of her youth: 'I didn't get into any [trouble]. That's the most boring thing in the entire world.'[8]

And so qualities like reliability, integrity and respect are all, with a cursory sentence, tossed in a skip called 'boring'.

The word 'goodness' invokes images of prissy, puritanical, legalistic souls. One online dictionary defines a 'do-gooder' as a 'naive idealist who supports philanthropic or humanitarian causes or reforms'.[9]

The impression is clear: good people have just not been around the block enough to wise up and act like the rest of the voracious pack but, one of these days, they're going to shed their virginal innocence and get a life, suckers that they are.

We've even got a rather odd term for the constantly good.

Keira used it, tagging herself as 'absolutely a goody two-shoes'. According to urbandictionary.com a goody two-shoes is not just a nice person with, well, two shoes, but:

*A person (almost always a female) who tries to be as good and 'clean' as humanly possible. She is more often than not a staunch conservative and takes pride in her virginity and her practice of abstinence. She is definitely a God-fearing girl who always goes to church every Sunday, and indeed, based on the way she dresses, she looks like she's going to church every day. She cannot abide it when people [swear] in front of her – the most extreme goody two shoeses faint when hearing foul language*

*- and of course she would never consider smoking, drinking, doing drugs, or having any physical contact with a boy beyond holding hands or perhaps a kiss on the cheek. Can be nice but eventually begins to lecture you about your 'sinful' lifestyle and just becomes a pest.*[10]

And the same 'dictionary' relates words and phrases like 'prude', 'teacher's pet', 'sissy', 'snob' and 'prig' with the term. In an upside-down world, where being bad is celebrated, and being good is confessed, almost with shame, we need to affirm that being good is, well, good.

But what does that mean? Do we need to rediscover the goodness of goodness? Barnabas can help us with that.

-        -        -        -        -

Goodness. Surely it's about doing the right thing, living pure and clean, embracing honesty, even when nobody else is looking. And it's not just a privatised piety, goodness for the sake of personal virtue, but has a social element: we are called to be good for the benefit of others: praying for an enemy, volunteering in a food bank, giving generously to help alleviate poverty.

But as we zoom in on Barnabas, meeting with the new believers in Antioch - hearing their stories of how they found faith in Christ, weeping with them as they describe their pressures because of their new allegiance to Him, consoling them over their failures - we see a beautiful aspect of goodness that is often overlooked.

# Barnabas was a good man, because he had an open heart and an open mind.

William Barclay, the famed commentator, calls Barnabas the 'man with the biggest heart in the Church',[11] and for good reason. The word 'good' speaks of a liberal mindedness that meant that Barnabas was willing to think, as it were, outside the box. Even though what was happening in Antioch was absolutely groundbreaking, and Barnabas was entering into a new theological paradigm, nevertheless he saw that God Himself was graciously at work. Barnabas possessed a combination of spiritual discernment and an open heart.

The new converts lived in Antioch, which means that their lifestyles would most likely have still needed a lot of revision. But Barnabas didn't pick on what was wrong, but celebrated what was right. He hunted for grace to commend, and didn't go searching for flaws to amplify and condemn. As R. Kent Hughes wrote:

> Barnabas could easily have seen the situation in a different light. These people were new, untaught Christians. They still carried the mire of Antioch with them. Some of them had miles to go in their language and relationships and ethics. But Barnabas 'saw the evidence of the grace of God.' He could see Christian grace and charm in their lives – the fruit of the Spirit: 'love, joy, peace ...' – and 'he was glad.' So he simply 'encouraged them all to remain true to the Lord with all their hearts,' to meditate on him, to make him everything!
>     In this way Barnabas helped them focus on that which would cleanse them of the defilement of Antioch.[12]

Sometimes we can be blinded to the grace of God at work in others because of prejudice. We don't see much good in them because we first notice the negative, which we then choose to focus on. Before long we are tempted to write them off, categorising them as bad people, oblivious to very real character strengths that they have. As a Jew from a Levite background, Barnabas would have been schooled in the idea that the Gentile world was effectively outside the covenantal work of God. But he refused to allow his past thinking to influence his attitude to what was happening in the Golden City. And joy and celebration was the result - he was glad.

'Good' can also mean 'safe'. And so it would have been very easy for Barnabas to play it safe, and demand that the Gentile converts in Antioch initially submit to Jewish rules until the emerging questions had been answered. But instead of leaning towards legalism, the man who was glad because he *saw* grace, made others glad as he *shared* grace. At this stage of his ministry, he boldly encouraged the new converts to simply 'remain true to the Lord with all their hearts' (Acts 11:23). Rather than placing huge importance on external ceremony, he chose to validate them because of their heartfelt love for Christ, and their desire to be faithful to Him.

# Legalism is a virus that can attack us all.

It starts when we insist that everyone does faith our way, and that our personal principles are universal. While there are obviously absolute standards that Scripture holds up as unchanging, let's be careful to make sure that we're not making disciples in our own image, but seeking to help them to look like Jesus. And that might mean erring on the side of grace.

Goodness is not just about behaviour, how we act, but being good in who we are. This phrase, 'full of faith and of the Holy Spirit', is a favourite of Dr Luke's as he writes Acts. He uses the same phrase to describe Stephen, the brave martyr (see Acts 6:5). We're pointed to a vital truth here - being 'good' is not just about being thoroughly nice people as a result of our own efforts, but is the result of being steadily transformed as we co-operate with the Holy Spirit who works in us daily. Just as a tree has no power to produce blossom without the sap rising within it, so true and deep character change takes place in us as the Holy Spirit produces good fruit in our lives.

Our hearts need the surgical work of the Spirit of God in order that we might truly do that which humans find so hard to do – change.

Christians have argued for centuries about exactly what is involved in being filled with the Holy Spirit. Some argue – I think wrongly – that speaking in tongues is the 'initial evidence' of being Spirit-filled. While speaking in tongues is a wonderful gift – I have it and am grateful for it – surely there were other evidences within Barnabas' life that showed God's Spirit being at work in and through him. His open-hearted attitude, coupled with goodness, kindness and generosity – all these characteristics were in him because God's Spirit filled him. There were further evidences too, including faith. As we realise our need for God daily – the Bible tells us literally to go on being 'filled with the Spirit' (Eph. 5:18) – a continuous experience rather than a one-time event – so our capacity for trusting God increases. And it seems that Barnabas was something of a catalyst for the ongoing growth of the Church, as Luke quickly adds that a great number of people were brought to the Lord.

Goodness. It's not about being a staunch, ramrod-upright crusader.

It's not about narrow-minded tunnel vision.

It's what's needed whenever God does something new, something historic, as He did in the grimy city of Antioch.

# There's nothing dull about goodness. It's truly spectacular.

And good people tell the truth about faith.

And the truth is, the pathway of faith can be difficult to navigate.

And in Antioch, life was very tough for the Christians.

-        -        -        -        -

Gentiles were turning to Jesus in large numbers in Antioch, but that growth was happening despite increasing pressure there. The Jesus people in Antioch were suffering. Refugees, they were objects of derision because of their faith in Christ. The term 'Christian' probably began with negative connotations. Antioch was famous for cutting humour and giving tongue-in-cheek nicknames. When a group of fanatical followers of the Emperor Nero did some cheerleading in support of their hero and god, they were dubbed the *Augustiani*. So, in an attempt to mock the Christ followers, some called them the *Christianoi*. The Christians. The sarcastic citizens of Antioch had no idea that the name would stick.

And then there were further threats on the horizon, specifically from the Emperor I just mentioned, the infamous Nero. A young man, he was born in AD 37, so was only five years old at this time. However, he would rise to power early, just twelve years after Barnabas went to investigate the wonderful grace happenings at Antioch.

History informs us that Nero was fair haired, had a fat neck, was covered in spots and smelt very bad.[13] More ominously, he tried, unsuccessfully, to poison his mother. When that failed he rigged the ceiling above her bed to collapse (that failed too) and then he sunk a ship that she was on. She, apparently like a cat with many lives, survived as she swam ashore. Finally he had her assassinated.

THERE ARE NO ORDINARY PEOPLE

Nero loved being on stage. Nobody was allowed to leave during his performances – some women gave birth during them, and men pretended to die so they could be carried out. Apparently he wasn't the greatest actor or singer.

But he was a pathological, amoral murderer who launched a period of state-sanctioned persecution that would last for 300 years. Christians would be terribly tortured and then set on fire, used as scapegoats for the great fire of Rome of AD 64. According to tradition, four years later the apostle Paul would be beheaded in Rome under Nero's watch.

All of this pain was on the immediate horizon when Barnabas visited Antioch.

# His message about holding on to God was prophetic and timely.

They had pain to come, and they were already experiencing pressure and ridicule. They had come through the fire of the Jerusalem persecution and subsequent scattering.

But in their pain we read a very telling statement – that the 'Lord's hand was with them' (Acts 11:21). This imagery is rooted in the Old Testament. The 'hand of the Lord' is a favourite term of Dr Luke's: he speaks of God's hand being with John the Baptist (Luke 1:66), with the apostles in providing miracles (Acts 4:30) and against Elymas the sorcerer in judgment (Acts 13:11). They were suffering, but blessed, and so Barnabas encouraged them to 'remain true to the Lord with all their hearts' (Acts 11:23).

He didn't promise an end to their trouble, but affirmed that there would be endless faithfulness from the Jesus who would always be with them.

—    —    —    —    —

It would be a life message from Barnabas.

# Hang on tight to God. Endure.

Later, it would be the message that Barnabas helped bring to the new Christians in another Antioch, this time in Pisidia:

> *Barnabas, who talked with them and urged them to continue in the grace of God.*
>
> (Acts 13:43)

And then again:

> *Then they returned to Lystra, Iconium and Antioch, strengthening the disciples and encouraging them to remain true to the faith. 'We must go through many hardships to enter the kingdom of God,' they said.*
>
> (Acts 14:21-22)

We've already seen that Barnabas was a consummate encourager.

# But the essence of encouragement is not a blithe suggestion that everything is going to be alright.

I recall the pain that was inflicted upon some friends of ours by that kind of thoughtless 'encouragement'. Their son was spiralling down into a destructive lifestyle centred on drug and alcohol abuse. He had been arrested a number of times and had been so close to an overdose that they feared for his life. One night, in a small group setting, they tearfully asked for prayer. A well-meaning couple, whose children had never been through any times of rebellion or dysfunctional behaviour, tried to reassure them. 'Don't worry', they said, 'it will be alright'.

On the way home, the anxious parents reflected that they were grateful for the care shown by their friends, but not appreciative of the hollow words they had shared. How did they know that everything was going to turn out alright? Life doesn't always work like that, and encouragement begins to sound empty if it is simply rooted in wishful thinking. But we want to believe that the good result will always come, that the test will surely be negative, that the circumstance we fear won't unfold. But sometimes it does, no matter how hard we pray, no matter how much we trust.

Barnabas refused to offer any pain-free guarantees; instead he assured his new friends that hardship was part of the thorny pathway of life – and, especially in their context of religious persecution, times would be harder for kingdom people.

Let's encourage each other, not with wishful thinking, but with what we know is sure – that God is concerned, that He hears our prayers and that He is actively involved. Let's promise each other that God will never abandon us. But let's not give assurances that there will be no hardship ahead.

# Good people tell the truth about faith.

And Christianity is often about simply clinging on to faith for dear life.

# Nine:
## INVEST IN THE BIGGEST LOSERS

*'Then Barnabas went to Tarsus to look for Saul, and when he found him, he brought him to Antioch. So for a whole year Barnabas and Saul met with the church and taught great numbers of people. The disciples were called Christians first at Antioch.*

*During this time some prophets came down from Jerusalem to Antioch. One of them, named Agabus, stood up and through the Spirit predicted that a severe famine would spread over the entire Roman world. (This happened during the reign of Claudius.) The disciples, as each one was able, decided to provide help for the brothers and sisters living in Judea. This they did, sending their gift to the elders by Barnabas and Saul.' - Acts 11:25-30*

*'When Barnabas and Saul had finished their mission, they returned from[1] Jerusalem, taking with them John, also called Mark.'*
*- Acts 12:25*

*'What is more, I consider everything a loss because of the surpassing worth of knowing Christ Jesus my Lord, for whose sake I have lost all things.' - Philippians 3:8*

'You can either light a fire underneath people or you can light a fire within them' - Anon.[2]

'The glory of friendship is not the outstretched hand, nor the kindly smile nor the joy of companionship; it is the spiritual inspiration that comes to one when he discovers that someone else believes in him and is willing to trust him.' - Ralph Waldo Emerson[3]

'Truly great friends are hard to find, difficult to leave, and impossible to forget.' - Anon.[4]

'Don't make friends who are comfortable to be with. Make friends who will force you to lever yourself up.' - Thomas J. Watson[5]

Nearly a decade had passed since their fateful meeting with the elders in Jerusalem, when Barnabas had stepped up, taken a risk and vouched for Saul. Following that encounter, the relatively newly converted Saul had found himself in hot water very quickly and, after an initial period of preaching, had returned to his native city of Tarsus.

Nothing is known about his time there. These are known as Saul's silent years. No church was planted in Tarsus. Some, perhaps eager to paint Saul in a positive light, insist that he continued preaching, although there is no specific record of it. Some commentators say that, during this period, Saul was repeatedly beaten by synagogue officials, perhaps as a result of preaching in Cilician synagogues. It's possible that his comment about going 'to Syria and Cilicia' (Gal. 1:21) is evidence that he was functioning as an intolerant preacher. Others suggest that he was disinherited by his family during this difficult season.

Still others speculate that during this time he had the ecstatic experience of being caught up to the third heaven (2 Cor. 12:1-4).

What we do know is this: Saul had become a complete loser. In 2 Corinthians 11:23-28 he is basically summing up his situation as:

I've lost everything. All things.

He had lost the status and power that was his as an anti-Christian zealot and persecutor.

He'd lost safety and security, having had to run for his life and get out of Jerusalem fast because of a death threat.

He'd lost the foundations and moorings that his Jewish faith had given him, and was having to navigate uncharted territory as a follower of Jesus.

He'd lost the community of friends and even family as those who had once loved and respected him turned their backs on him.

# The biggest loser.

In contrast, Barnabas had been winning, experiencing great success in leading the church in Antioch, but was at this point struggling. Apparently the mushrooming church in Antioch was making demands upon him that he just could not meet. Most likely the needs of a growing church were proving too much for one man. He needed help, and not simply help from God. Barnabas needed someone to partner with him in leadership and ministry.

-        -        -        -        -

It's one of those verses that are so often quoted completely out of context: 'I can do all things through Christ who strengthens me' (Phil. 4:13, NKJV). The implication is that we can do anything – all things. But we can't. I can't play the bassoon, speak Cantonese or give birth. I can only do that which Christ calls me to, and therefore strengthens me for.

It's important that we hear this. The language of the Church is often focused on stepping out, expanding our spheres, being stretched, being developed, being more than we are now. But we don't hear enough about establishing and affirming the God-given limitations that are ours because of the gifts that we have, or don't have.

# We need to know what we can do, what we should perhaps try and what we certainly cannot do.

I know. I used to lead worship, guitar in hand. Now, I don't. In order to discover what I could do best, I had to acknowledge what I wasn't terribly good at.

Trust me. When I sang, people would cry out to God.

In pain.

Barnabas, so successful, so established and respected, needed some assistance, and he was humble enough to admit it.

And he thought he knew just the right man for the job.

-     -     -     -     -

Finding Saul was no easy task. For one thing, Antioch to Tarsus was a major journey of some 150 miles, nothing today, but a significant trek back then. And then when he arrived in the city, Barnabas had to track Saul down. When Luke says that Barnabas 'looked' for Saul, he uses a word that means to search high and low, until, after some considerable difficulty, the person is finally located. If Saul had been disinherited, this might explain some of the challenge. No longer living with his family, perhaps he was living in quiet anonymity.

So why did Barnabas go to such incredible lengths to find Saul, and then persuade him to give up his life in Tarsus and relocate to Antioch to become co-leader there?

Obviously someone with an openness to the surprising grace of God was needed. Saul had experienced that – but then the leaders back in Jerusalem had taken some convincing of his conversion. So perhaps Barnabas concluded that a candidate from Jerusalem wouldn't be ideal, but a man like Saul – who himself had experienced such outrageous grace – would be perfect for the task.

But there was most likely another reason.

We've already seen that Barnabas listened to and was able to rehearse Saul's conversion story. And that story would have included a pivotal episode in Saul's life.

A man called Ananias had been clearly told by God that not only was Saul a genuine convert, or that he would be a great leader, but that he would be the primary voice to bring the gospel to the Gentiles.

> But the Lord said to Ananias, 'Go! This man is my chosen instrument to proclaim my name to the Gentiles and their kings and to the people of Israel.'
>
> (Acts 9:15)

And back in Antioch, the converts there were mostly from a Gentile background.

Based on the prophetic insight of Ananias, it was obvious to Barnabas that Saul was the man to help out in Antioch.

Although he couldn't know the full implications of it then, Barnabas was leading Saul to a situation where his ministry would not just change that dark city, but would change the world. Just as Barnabas had led him into vital connection in Jerusalem, so once again God's plan was quietly unfolding as Barnabas took Saul to Antioch. This was a partnership for destiny.

Antioch was an internship for Saul. There he learned how to invest in the local church, to consistently teach. His sharp, lawyer-like mind perfectly complemented Barnabas' pastoral gifts.

Perhaps Saul thought that he was simply going from A to B – from Tarsus to Antioch. He might have even speculated that he would fully fulfil his ministry to the Gentiles through serving that local church. But, whether he knew it or not, the world was waiting.

Sometimes we need to allow God to show us the limitations of our spheres and gifts, as Barnabas had to acknowledge in seeking help.

We must know that often God leads us to a situation that is just a bridge to our wider calling.

And we also need to allow God to shatter our perceived limits, as Saul would eventually discover – with Barnabas' help.

# We all know that we need friends.

Just as Barnabas encouraged the believers in Antioch to hold tight to God, so his influence in Saul's life nudged Saul to fulfil his calling, and to pursue Christ with passion. Barnabas was a door opener for Saul. And, as we'll see, he would be willing to disagree with his ministry partner when the need arose.

Let's see that our friendships are part of God's
provision, not only for our comfort, but to help
us discover all that God has for us.

Saul needed God's call. And he needed
God's connector in his life.

Barnabas.

-        -        -        -        -

I wonder what was going through Barnabas' mind as the
pair walked the final few miles to Antioch. A congregation
of people now known as 'Christians' awaited them there.
Barnabas was about to introduce them to their new leader.

And that new leader, Saul, was quite possibly
the most unlikely candidate on earth.

In Antioch, there were people in the community there who
would have viewed Saul as a big loser - but not because
of the price he'd paid for Christ, but because of the price
they'd paid due to his terrible work as a persecutor.

The persecutor was becoming the pastor.

Actually, it was far more radical than that.

# Their persecutor was becoming their pastor.

Many in the congregation in Antioch were in the city because
of the terrible persecution that had taken place when Stephen
was killed - and we've seen that Saul, in his pre-Christian days,
was one of the primary architects of that persecution. Because
of this man, many of the believers in Antioch may have lost
homes, livelihoods and even loved ones. Now he was not

only joining their church, but becoming a teacher and leader. This is epic grace shown – and Dr Luke doesn't even point it out; rather, grace is demonstrated without fanfare or fuss.

Let's realise that the Church is not a community of similar, like-minded people who naturally get along, but is rather a gathering of diverse souls who would find no connection whatsoever except at the unifying cross of Jesus. And the gift of encouragement that Barnabas possessed helped cement people together who otherwise might have been in horrible conflict – such as Saul and the Antioch congregation.

Why was Saul accepted without apparent question?

Surely it was because the Antioch church had learned to trust Barnabas. He had blessed them with endorsement and trust when they'd claimed conversion.

Now, upon his recommendation, they would do what seemed impossible, and accept their former enemy as a leader among them.

And the trust they invested in Saul was full, extending even to the use of their money.

A trusted prophet, Agabus – he appears twice in Saul's life with significant prophetic instruction (see Acts 21:10-11) – prophesied about a coming famine in Judea. The famine there would be especially severe – 'the Jewish historian Josephus records that many people died for lack of money to buy what little food was available.'[6] This was an extremely serious economic crisis, and the Church was quick to respond, an amazingly sacrificial act from a group of people who themselves had lost so much. But notice that encourager Barnabas and his assistant Saul were the ones fully entrusted to carry the gift to the church in Judea (Acts 11:30).

–      –      –      –      –

The Early Church was, at this point, facing a critical turning point in history: Saul was about to be fully recognised as an apostle to the Gentiles, sent out by the church at Antioch together with his companion Barnabas.

The way had been prepared by Stephen as he laid down his life for the gospel, and Philip, who had gone to an Ethiopian and to the Samaritans with the message.

The church in Antioch had been born because exiles from the Jerusalem persecution had gossiped the gospel as they fled, and Greek-speaking Gentiles had come to faith in that city. But up until now all the evangelising had been limited to the Syrian and Palestinian mainland, with the exception of Cyprus, which is mentioned earlier (Acts 11:19).

But the breathtaking moment when world mission was birthed was about to happen.

-        -        -        -        -

Picture Barnabas on the long trek to Tarsus from Antioch.

# Investing in others is hard work. It takes time, effort, risk, self-sacrifice, money.

Many of us have no significant, resourcing and veteran friendships because we've been unwilling to pay that price.

Look at Barnabas again, trudging along the long road to Tarsus, and then searching high and low in the city, unwilling to give up until he'd tracked down his long-lost friend.

His investment was about to pay off.

For himself, because he was about to form a dynamic partnership and friendship.

For the church in Antioch, because they were to benefit from the ministry of the dynamic, intellectual colossus that was Saul.

And, although Barnabas could not know it, his investment was about to pay off for the wider world. Millions of believers would be affected by the trek to Tarsus, including you and me.

# Investment in big losers can bring massive wins.

# Ten:
## TUNE IN TO MIDDLE C

*'When Barnabas and Saul had finished their mission, they returned from Jerusalem, taking with them John, also called Mark. Now in the church at Antioch there were prophets and teachers: Barnabas, Simeon called Niger, Lucius of Cyrene, Manaen (who had been brought up with Herod the tetrarch) and Saul. While they were worshipping the Lord and fasting, the Holy Spirit said, "Set apart for me Barnabas and Saul for the work to which I have called them." So after they had fasted and prayed, they placed their hands on them and sent them off.' – Acts 12:25-13:3*

'The really good news for humanity is that Jesus is now taking students in the master class of life. The eternal life that begins with confidence in Jesus is a life in his present kingdom, now on earth and available to all. So the message of and about him is specifically a gospel for our life now, not just for dying. It is about living now as his apprentice in kingdom living, not just as a consumer of his merits. Our future, however far we look, is a natural extension of the faith by which we live now and the life in which we now participate. Eternity is now in flight and we with it, like it or not.' – Dallas Willard[1]

'Reverence and awe have often been replaced by a yawn of familiarity. The consuming fire has been domesticated into a candle flame, adding a bit of religious atmosphere, perhaps, but no heat, no blinding light, no power for purification.' – Donald McCullough[2]

'When we stay focused on the Jesus we meet in the New Testament, we discover no "gentle Jesus, meek and mild", but one who grabs us by the scruff of the neck to shake loose from us all false images of deity we have cherished, one who is the great iconoclast smashing to bits our trivial gods.' – Donald McCullough[3]

'Of course we must be "born again" individually; not as orphans, however, but as members of God's congregational family. At the same time we must not rush to the opposite extreme and become so enthusiastic about corporate and congregational applications of scripture that we neglect, or underemphasise, the necessity of individual faith and a personal walk with Christ ... we need to emphasise the corporate alongside the personal.' – Michael Griffiths[4]

*Groundhog Day* is the story of Phil Connors, played by
Bill Murray. Connors is a self-centred, sarcastic television
weatherman who covers the annual Groundhog Day festival
in Punxsutawney, Pennsylvania. Connors despises the whole
event, believing it to be unworthy of his time. After filming his
piece to camera, Connors and his director, Rita, are caught in a
giant blizzard (which he fails to predict) and are forced to stay
in town. When he wakes up the next morning, something very
strange has happened – it's 2 February all over again, as it is the
next morning, and every morning thereafter. Connors comes to
believe that whatever he does, there will be no consequences – it
will always be 2 February – and so he throws himself into crime,
materialism, money, sex – all of which leaves him unfulfilled.
He falls for Rita, but can't manipulate her to love him back, and
finally says (in what sounds amazingly like a pre-conversion
statement), 'I've come to the end of me. There's no way out now.'

Phil commits suicide – only to wake up on
2 February once more. Life is forever the same.

Connors confides in Rita and tells her what's going
on. As he speaks, he tosses cards into a hat, and she
comments, 'So *this* is what you do with eternity.'

Realising that life is not just about idle play, Connors
turns to art, poetry, music, sculpture, and pours
himself into serving the community that he despised,
Punxsutawney. He reaches out, comes to really know
and be known, and is finally fulfilled: he is reborn.[5]

We can live *Groundhog Day* ourselves. I'm not suggesting
that life is not predictable, that there are not duties to fulfil
every day, some of which are routine and even dull. But
there's a danger of us frittering 'eternity' away, assuming that
every day will essentially follow the same track as the one
before, without possibility of change or divine disruption.

Sometimes God calls us to a radical reorientation of our priorities, or even a cataclysmic change for the better – even though the change seems incredibly risky.

# And that can be true, even if life is going along rather well.

-    -    -    -    -

In Antioch, the church was thriving.

The decision that Barnabas took to recruit reclusive Saul into co-leadership there was proven to be right. Luke records a wonderful twelve-month season of growth:

> *So for a whole year Barnabas and Saul met with the church and taught great numbers of people.*
>
> (Acts 11:26)

In a way, Barnabas and Saul were just getting started.

But then two incidents happened. The first we mentioned in the last chapter: the Antiochene church heard about a need created by famine, and responded to it by sending their two primary leaders off to Jerusalem with a gift.

That radical decision shows what kind of leadership Barnabas and Saul exercised: they made themselves totally replaceable.

The journey from Antioch to Jerusalem was a round trip of some 800 miles, so this meant that, at the very least, the two senior leaders would be absent from their home church for at least two to three months.

Having completed their mission, they returned, probably anticipating digging in for a further season of investment and leadership in Antioch.

But it was not to be.

# God had other ideas.
# He often does.

If we're to live heroically, we need to abandon the idea that God is a heavenly adviser, consultant or coach.

He is not any of those.

He is God, the One in charge and He frequently gives commands, because that is what God does. Speaking at a commencement address at Duke University in 1987, newscaster Ted Koppel reminded his audience:

> *What Moses brought down from [Mt.] Sinai*
> *were not the Ten Suggestions*[6]

But a consumerist approach to faith can lead us to think that God is an adviser, who would never demand anything costly from us. That notion is exemplified by some self-help spirituality. One lady, called Sheila, has created her own religion, Sheilaism.

> *I believe in God. I'm not a religious fanatic.*
> *I can't remember the last time I went to*
> *church. My faith has carried me a long way.*
> *It's Sheilaism. Just my own little voice.*[7]

None of us are immune from this human tendency to try to make God into what we'd like Him to be, rather than allow Him to be who He is.

Sociologist Émile Durkheim said:

> *Every tribe/society invents a god who reflects its*
> *values, standards, aspirations, hopes, ambitions*
> *and attitudes and then worships it – thus*
> *legitimating its own standards of behavior.*[8]

In other words, we can be tempted to want a god (God) who blesses us, helps us, cheers us up when we're down and does what we want him (Him) to do.

But God is God. He speaks, and calls us to align ourselves with His command. But if that is to become a reality, we must know that constant tuning is called for.

- - - - -

In a previous book (now out of print), I shared a story told by Lloyd C. Douglas, who wrote the novel, *The Robe*. Douglas described a friendship with a retired music teacher whom he met while in university. They lived in the same lodgings, the older man disabled and unable to leave his ground-floor apartment. A daily ritual of sorts developed between them; every morning Douglas would open the old man's door and ask the same question: 'Well, what's the good news?' The older gentleman would pick up his tuning fork, tap it on the metal arm of his wheelchair, and respond:

> *That's middle C! It was middle C yesterday; it will be middle C tomorrow; it will be middle C a thousand years from now. The tenor upstairs sings flat, the piano across the hall is out of tune, but that, my friend, is middle C'*[9]

# God is the 'middle C' of the universe, the magnificent, faithful holy One.

If we are to live heroically, and avoid lash-ups of epic proportions, then we need to learn to tune in to His voice.

He still talks.

But let's be honest.

Often when we hear another Christian announce
that God has spoken to them we cringe, because too
many mad ideas have been attributed to the Lord.

'The Lord told me' is a phrase that has licensed harebrained
schemes, weirdly impossible dreams and ineffective causes.
Using that phrase, Christians insist that their preferences
are God's preferences, move church without real reason
and change marriage partners. It's a phrase often used by
those who are unwilling to have a difficult conversation
with their fellow humans: when we announce that God has
spoken, that effectively silences any disagreeable dialogue.

But even though some prophecies aren't remotely prophetic,
and some revelations are little more than the fruit of too
much cheese before bed, coupled with some wishful
thinking, the truth is this: God does still speak. But if we are
to hear and heed Him, we need to consciously tune in.

-         -         -         -         -

# How do we tune in?

One important truth for us to know is that availability to God
doesn't imply irresponsibility. History is littered with half-finished
projects or people abandoning God-given commissions because
something more interesting came along, and God supposedly
spoke. Notice eagle-eyed Luke's attention to a vital detail –
Barnabas and Saul have returned to Antioch having completed
their mission. The Greek in the original text is somewhat
cumbersome, because Luke is at pains to tell us that not only have
they come back to the Golden City, but they have returned having
fully accomplished all that they were sent out to do, as they were
dispatched earlier with the offering to provide famine relief.

Notice that the call came when the church was gathered together in worship and fasting, deliberately seeking God. In an individualistic culture, where often our preferences are viewed as paramount, it may come as a bit of a jolt to discover that calling comes in the context of commitment not only to church, but to a church that is hungrily pursuing the purposes of God as they practise the spiritual disciplines together.

And then there will often be a huge step of faith when God speaks, partly because He doesn't always give details or outcomes when He calls.

When the Holy Spirit spoke at Antioch, the word was simply, 'Set apart for me Barnabas and Saul for the work to which I have called them' (Acts 13:2).

Question: what work is that, exactly?

We're not told, and perhaps they weren't told either.

The only calling that we've previously heard about was Saul's calling to the Gentiles, confirmed by Ananias, which we touched on briefly earlier.

As far as we know, Barnabas had not had a specific calling to go to the Gentiles prior to this specific Holy Spirit-inspired commissioning in Antioch. He had 'bumped into' his calling to the Gentiles as a delegate previously sent from Jerusalem.

Some people have distinct, repeatedly confirmed callings, like Saul.

Others discover their destiny as they obediently put one foot in front of another each day, and then, as they continue, God grants confirmation of their calling, like Barnabas.

# However God calls, His calling comes to those who are available and endeavouring to listen.

Barnabas and Paul were engaged in corporate fasting and worship (Jesus' teaching on private fasting doesn't condemn corporate fasting, but rather insists that we don't use fasting as a badge of pride - see Matt. 6:16-18). Although the instruction to set the two apart for apostolic mission came from the Holy Spirit, the dynamic duo, together with the rest of the congregation there, received that directive while they were giving themselves to those spiritual disciplines. The inference is that the Word of the Lord came through the prophets in the church. Encourager Barnabas didn't just live his life by doing good and noble things; he was available and obedient to God, and obeyed the Holy Spirit in embracing a call that was costly and disruptive.

Frankly, I'm not a great fan of fasting. I prefer feasting. But I'm challenged to pick up that neglected discipline in my life - not to be legalistic, but to express my ongoing availability to whatever God wants from me.

Let's not waste a second of the eternity that is already in flight.

God is a music maker. When He plays middle C, let's tune ourselves to that perfect note.

# Eleven:
## BEWARE OF SLURRED SPEECH

*'The two of them, sent on their way by the Holy Spirit, went down to Seleucia and sailed from there to Cyprus. When they arrived at Salamis, they proclaimed the word of God in the Jewish synagogues. John was with them as their helper.*

*They travelled through the whole island until they came to Paphos. There they met a Jewish sorcerer and false prophet named Bar-Jesus, who was an attendant of the proconsul, Sergius Paulus. The proconsul, an intelligent man, sent for Barnabas and Saul because he wanted to hear the word of God. But Elymas the sorcerer (for that is what his name means) opposed them and tried to turn the proconsul from the faith.' - Acts 13:4-8*

'There are two equal and opposite errors into which our race can fall about the devils. One is to disbelieve in their existence. The other is to believe, and to feel an excessive and unhealthy interest in them. They themselves are equally pleased by both errors and hail a materialist or a magician with the same delight.' - C.S. Lewis[1]

'I think the devil doesn't exist, but man has created him, he has created him in his own image and likeness.' – Fyodor Dostoyevsky[2]

'I now know Satan is real. I have met it.'
– M. Scott Peck[3]

'A sense of desperation has come upon some of us. We cannot cope with certain problems that we have been faced with clinically. The people with these problems make little response to our professional ingenuity. Perhaps we have missed something quite important both psychologically and spiritually because we have ignored the material in the Bible about Satan and the demonic.' – Basil Jackson[4]

'A mighty fortress is our God,
A bulwark never failing;
Our helper he amid the flood
of mortal ills prevailing:
For still our ancient foe doth
seek to work us woe;
His craft and power are great
and armed with cruel hate,
On earth is not his equal ...
The prince of darkness grim –
We tremble not for him;
His rage we can endure,

For, lo! His doom is sure.' - Martin Luther[5]


In some portraits, he has horns. Hoofs. A tail. An impish smirk, and a goatee. His eyebrows arch mischievously.

He carries a pitchfork.

He can't stand music.

And it seems he is allergic to ink.

I'm talking, of course, about the devil.

In the Middle Ages the image of a horned, tailed, hoofed and hairy Satan with bat wings became popular.

But for some, the cartoon character - not remotely rooted in the biblical description of him - had made Satan into just that; a fictional cartoon figure, up there with Peter Pan and the Wizard of Oz.

That's not to say that Satan, as a character, has vanished from popular consciousness.

Hollywood, responding to the popular thirst for movies in the horror/supernatural genre, endlessly draws our attention to devils and demons. When *The Exorcist* hit our cinemas back in 1973, it launched a string of devil-centred shock flicks. Earning over a quarter of a billion dollars, it's still one of the highest earning 'R' rated (18) films in history.

It seems Hollywood has taken Satan and reduced him to being a scary, terrifying, powerful - but nevertheless fictional - character, even though *The Exorcist* was based on true events that happened in 1949, when an exorcism was performed on a young boy from Cottage City, Maryland, by Jesuit priest, Fr William S. Bowdern.

The 1976 book, *Hostage to the Devil*, by former Jesuit priest, Malachi Martin, became a Book of the Month Club main selection. It describes five cases of demonic possession and successful exorcisms. In the late 1980s, talk-show host Geraldo Rivera featured Satanism on a controversial but widely viewed television special.[6]

But in some circles, when people declare that they believe there is a real character called Satan, there is a reaction ranging from a nervous titter to outright ridicule.

Rick Santorum, a US presidential contender back in 2012, made headlines when he professed a belief that there is a figure called Satan. During a speech at a Catholic university, Santorum warned that Satan had his 'sights on' America:

> *Satan [has been] attacking the great institutions of America, using those great vices of pride, vanity and sensuality as the root to attack all of the strong plants that [have] been so deeply rooted in the American tradition.*[7]

There was an immediate reaction, notably from a professor of a Divinity School, C. Melissa Snarr, associate professor of ethics and society at Vanderbilt University:

> *Santorum's comments regarding his theory of the fall of American institutions is, I think, quite relevant in the current presidential debate. In a public speech, Santorum offered a grand interpretation of the current challenges facing the United States. I think it is imperative to analyze and debate his version of a political theodicy (or why bad things happen to good countries) and ask whether his interpretation is one that voters should feel comfortable backing.*[8]

Snarr then qualified her comments:

*[Santorum's] public political theology should be discussed thoroughly. This is not to say, however, that a belief in Satan or even spiritual warfare puts him at the 'extreme' end of Christianity. Belief in Satan and Satan's activity is present in multiple Christian traditions and particularly important for more theologically conservative evangelical believers – of whom there are many in the U.S.*[9]

*Newsweek* magazine insists that Satan has been 'debunked by rationalists, exorcized by psychotherapists, and demythologised by theologians'.[10] There is no devil in the detail, or anywhere else: that's the suggestion.

And this is not just a trend that is developing outside of the Church. In a survey conducted in 2009, four out of ten Christians (40 per cent) strongly agreed that Satan 'is not a living being but is a symbol of evil'. An additional two out of ten Christians (19 per cent) said they 'agree somewhat' with that perspective. A minority of Christians indicated that they believe Satan is real by disagreeing with the statement: one-quarter (26 per cent) disagreed strongly and about one-tenth (9 per cent) disagreed somewhat. The remaining 6 per cent were not sure what they believe about the existence of Satan.[11]

Here I confess that, in my lifetime, my clarity about spiritual warfare in general, and the existence of an actual figure called Satan specifically, has eroded somewhat.

We are all pendulums, reacting constantly, especially to extremes.

In my early days in ministry, I read books and attended conferences and heard teaching that suggested that it was extremely easy to pick up a resident demon or two: demons could invade your life through specific sins, but also through nothing that you were responsible for: the circumstances of your birth, or some deviancy committed

by your great-great-great grandfather could apparently
set you up as an ideal landing strip for dark forces.

Looking back, I smile and mostly weep about this now. In one
church that I knew, a very fine young man committed suicide,
subjecting himself to an agonising death, partly because
of an over-emphasis on spiritual warfare in his church.

# I am also tired of people insisting that 'the devil made them do it' when caught in failure and sin.

One writer, Anthony Buzzard, dispatches that notion:

> We cannot blame Satan for our errors, claiming that 'the
> Devil made me do it.' We are responsible, with God's
> help, for learning the Truth, and turning from our sinful
> ways. The temptation which arises from the heart of
> man (James 1:14) and the evil thoughts which proceed
> 'from within, out of the heart of man' (Mark 7:21) may be
> prompted by Satan; they may also arise naturally, since
> human nature has been poisoned by the disobedience of
> Adam and Eve. But we must not confuse the evil which
> comes 'from within, out of the heart' with the Satan who
> comes up from the outside, as in the temptation story
> (Matt. 4). There is a close connection between sin and the
> original cause of sin, just as the conductor and the music
> he produces from an orchestra are connected. But no
> one would confuse the conductor with the orchestra.[12]

And so, in not wanting to focus on devilish activity, I
ignored it, and became almost oblivious to any thought
of dark schemes hatched to bring about my downfall.

But in so doing, I drifted away from a core belief that has
been held in the Church throughout the centuries.

Martin Luther, along with John Calvin, taught that there is a personal devil, one likely to despise music and song because 'he cannot stand gaiety'.[13] And it was Luther who attempted to 'chase away' Satan with some ink. Holed up for months while translating the Bible, one night he had a vision of Satan. Visitors to the castle of Wartburg can still see the damage caused by his hurled inkwell.

In my reactionary behaviour I found myself not so much sleeping with the enemy, but sleeping in the presence of the enemy, whereas Scripture clearly exhorts us to be very alert to satanic wiles and schemes. The apostle Peter offers a warning of warfare:

> *Be alert and of sober mind. Your enemy the devil prowls around like a roaring lion looking for someone to devour. Resist him, standing firm in the faith, because you know that the family of believers throughout the world is undergoing the same kind of sufferings.*

(1 Pet. 5:8-9)

James offers a similar warning:

> *Submit yourselves, then, to God. Resist the devil, and he will flee from you.*

(James 4:7)

The devil was certainly active in Cyprus when Barnabas and Paul began their wider ministry there. And his main tactic was devastatingly effective.

Slander.

Rumour mongering.

Slurs.

# Slurred speech. It's always been the devil's *modus operandi.*

-    -    -    -    -

The trip had been relatively uneventful.

Cyprus was such a pleasant place to be; some commentators have even suggested that John Mark, the young relative of Barnabas, went along on the trip because the location was so desirable.

Arriving in Salamis, the largest city of the island, Barnabas and Saul (soon to be called Paul by Luke)[14] began preaching in Jewish synagogues throughout the island, ending up in Paphos, which was a journey of around a hundred miles. No record is given of the response to their message, whether positive or negative. No reports of converts or persecutions.

But in Paphos, everything changed for the missionary duo.

Opportunity opened up for them, but, as is often the case, opposition came hard on the back of opportunity. The Roman governor of the island wanted to see Saul and Barnabas, keen to hear their message. But the pair were intercepted by a man who, according to his name, claimed to be a direct descendant of Jesus. He was a charlatan, who held the governor in his sway. Perhaps seeing Saul and Barnabas as a threat to his influence (and livelihood), the wizard of Cyprus did everything he could to persuade the governor to ignore them. That led to blinding judgment for the wizard - literally - but it demonstrates a strategy that Satan used during this first missionary journey: libel and lies.

It would be a repeated pattern:

In Paphos: 'But Elymas the sorcerer (for that is what his name means) opposed them and tried to turn the proconsul from the faith' (Acts 13:8).

In Pisidian Antioch: 'When the Jews saw the crowds, they were filled with jealousy. They began to contradict what Paul was saying and heaped abuse on him' (Acts 13:45).

And again: 'But the Jewish leaders incited the God-fearing women of high standing and the leading men of the city' (Acts 13:50).

In Iconium: 'But the Jews who refused to believe stirred up the other Gentiles and poisoned their minds against the brothers' (Acts 14:2).

In Lystra: 'Then some Jews came from Antioch and Iconium and won the crowd over' (Acts 14:19).

Slurred speech.

# Slurs about us, to us, about God. It's always been the way of the devil.

-　　-　　-　　-　　-

Satan consistently lies and slanders. Jesus wants to make that point clear, describing Satan not only as the liar but the father of lies (see John 8:44).

Satan accuses God, he accuses us. He makes fabricated offers, like the proffered deal in Eden (Gen. 3:5). He will lie to us about us, he'll lie to God about us (Zech. 3:1), he'll lie to us about God.

In a sense, he even lied to God about God, if you will, when he tried to divert Jesus from the kingdom plan that His Father sent Him to fulfil (Matt. 4:1-11).

He lies about sin and its consequences, airbrushing temptation with allure, so that only when we bite the apple do we discover the worm within.

# Countless Christians live their lives draped in shame, because they believe the whispers of the accuser.

They live feeling insignificant, because Satan has eroded their prophetic identity - the knowledge of who they are now, through grace, in Christ.

Churches are split and divided, because demonic forces have fuelled rumours and gossip.

Slurred speech.

If you want to live heroically, you'll come across opposition that will try to block your way, and, somewhere in the journey, you'll hear a whisper in your soul that tells you that whatever God wants you to do, you just can't.

Don't be preoccupied with Satan. But don't be ignorant of his schemes either.

# Twelve:
## GO FOR THE SILVER MEDAL

*'Then Saul, who was also called Paul, filled with the Holy Spirit, looked straight at Elymas and said, "You are a child of the devil and an enemy of everything that is right! You are full of all kinds of deceit and trickery. Will you never stop perverting the right ways of the Lord? Now the hand of the Lord is against you. You are going to be blind for a time, not even able to see the light of the sun."*

*Immediately mist and darkness came over him, and he groped about, seeking someone to lead him by the hand. When the proconsul saw what had happened, he believed, for he was amazed at the teaching about the Lord.*

*From Paphos, Paul and his companions sailed to Perga in Pamphylia, where John left them to return to Jerusalem.'*
*– Acts 13:9-13*

*'I wrote to the church, but Diotrephes, who loves to be first, will not welcome us.' – 3 John 1:9*

'[We are] obsessed with winning at everything. Often at any cost. It translates from the war rooms to the athletic fields to the top of the corporate ladder. Business language is infused with the vocabulary of the locker

room and battlefield. They battle to win in
a competitive market and dominate the
opposition with an aggressive plan, sometimes
"destroying their opponents."' – Ray Williams[1]

'Climb the mountain not to plant your
flag, but to embrace the challenge, enjoy
the air and behold the view. Climb it so
you can see the world, not so the world
can see you.' – David McCullough[2]

'Willingly accepting second billing is not very
much like what happens in our Christian
groups and churches, sad to say. If Barnabas
had forever taken front and center stage,
those who he had brought alongside him
would have continued to see themselves
as second-rate tools in God's hands, rusty
old blades instead of brand-new chainsaws.
Barnabas convinced them they had what
it takes to be in first place, even ahead of
an apostle such as himself.' – John Sloan[3]

It should have been one of the happiest days of their lives. To
stand aloft on the winner's podium in an Olympic Games is a
dream come true for any athlete, placing them at the pinnacle
of their chosen sport. To receive a medal, and then listen as
the national anthem – *your* nation's song – is played, and your
nation's flag is hoisted – surely it doesn't get any better than that.

Unless, of course, you win the silver medal, and stand
just a little lower than the person with the gold.

Photographers at the 2012 London Olympics catalogued the
facial expressions of those who came second, winning a silver
medal. Every picture tells a story, and it's surprising and sad.

Some silver medallists looked positively glum.
Annoyed. Tearful. Devastated. Even angry.

Michael Phelps and Ryan Lochte looked blue as they
stood among the members of the 4x100 freestyle relay
on 29 July. American gymnast McKayla Maroney made
no attempt to hide her disappointment at winning silver
after a tumble in the vault event robbed her of the number
one spot. Colombian cyclist Rigoberto Urán won silver
in the gruelling road race final but his furrowed-brow
frown speaks more of disappointment than triumph.

Perhaps the problem is that the silver medallists
came so very close to gold, which might explain why
psychologists discovered that bronze medal winners
appeared happier than those who took silver.[4]

Come first if you can. Sneak in with third place
if it's the best you can manage. But second
place is just too near to first for comfort.

Perhaps these downhearted medallists are just victims of the
prevailing notion that to truly be a winner, you have to be
the very, very best, fending off all competition. And when you
think like that, only gold will do. Only coming first will satisfy.

-       -       -       -       -

It's everywhere, the desperate, insatiable need to win, to climb the ladder to the uppermost rung, to be seen and applauded as the top dog.

It's viral in our culture, which so worships celebrity and fame. Store shelves are crammed with countless magazines chronicling the tedious tidbits of the glittery few: we devour details about their nights out, marital spats, fashion choices, dietary disciplines and divorces. We even have people who are famous for no other reason than the fact they're famous. But we are fickle and even unfaithful to our celebrity heroes. Many cheer when an unknown is suddenly catapulted into the nirvana of being known; some cheer louder when the famous topple and fall.

# The need to be seen, to be the best, infects faith and religion too.

Jesus reserved some of His strongest words of condemnation for those masters of show-and-tell religiosity, the Pharisees, who were addicted to taking the top spots when it came to personal piety:

> Be careful not to practice your righteousness in
> front of others to be seen by them. If you do, you
> will have no reward from your Father in heaven.
>    So when you give to the needy, do not announce it
> with trumpets, as the hypocrites do in the synagogues
> and on the streets, to be honoured by others.
> Truly I tell you, they have received their reward in full.
> (Matt. 6:1-2)
>
> And when you pray, do not be like the hypocrites,
> for they love to pray standing in the synagogues and

*on the street corners to be seen by others. Truly I*
*tell you, they have received their reward in full.*

(Matt. 6:5)

*When you fast, do not look sombre as the hypocrites do,*
*for they disfigure their faces to show others they are fasting.*
*Truly I tell you, they have received their reward in full.*

(Matt. 6:16)

*Everything they do is done for people to see:*
*they make their phylacteries wide and the tassels on*
*their garments long; they love the place of honour*
*at banquets and the most important seats in the*
*synagogues; they love to be greeted with respect in*
*the market-places and to be called 'Rabbi' by others.*

(Matt. 23:5-7)

And the desire for gold, to be celebrated as the
greatest, threatened Jesus' own team:

*They came to Capernaum. When he was in the house,*
*he asked them, 'What were you arguing about on*
*the road?' But they kept quiet because on the way*
*they had argued about who was the greatest.*
   *Sitting down, Jesus called the Twelve and*
*said, 'Anyone who wants to be first must be*
*the very last, and the servant of all.'*

(Mark 9:33-35)

The Bible tells the story of one man who, having occupied
the first chair for years, adjusted to stepping back,
allowing his protégé to take the more prominent role.

Barnabas again.

-     -     -     -     -

Barnabas had played a key, senior role of leadership in the Church for over eighteen years. He was recognised as a pivotal leader for four years before Saul had even been converted. He was by far the most experienced of the pair, and had been an influential member of what had initially been the headquarters church in Jerusalem while Saul was still a fire-breathing persecutor.

We've already seen that he was so respected, he'd been entrusted with the most delicate and sensitive of missions. Up until this point, Barnabas had been the acknowledged leader of the dynamic partnership between him and Saul.

Barnabas was the vintage disciple, whereas Saul was a relative newbie.

And then Barnabas was the senior partner in terms of ministry experience. He was the original pioneer of the church in Antioch.

# Barnabas had served as the primary door opener in Saul's life.

We recall that it was Barnabas who had initially vouched for Saul back in Jerusalem, and it was he who had opened the way for a year of fruitful ministry for Saul in Antioch.

Luke has a keen eye for detail, and he notes that when the Holy Spirit spoke, calling for the pair of old friends to be set apart for apostolic ministry, the phrase, 'Barnabas and Saul' was used (Acts 13:2). The tradition in biblical narrative is that the most important figure is named first.

Up until now, Luke always used that descriptor: Barnabas and Saul.

But now a transition, a succession was underway.

Saul was about to get his name changed to Paul, and begin to take a more prominent leadership role.

Paul and Barnabas.

Many preachers (including me) have mistakenly said that, from now on, it's always that way in the book of Acts: Paul listed before Barnabas.

That's not true. Look at what Luke says about the meeting that gathered in Jerusalem to discuss the contentious issue of Gentiles coming to faith in Christ:

> *The whole assembly became silent as they listened to Barnabas and Paul telling about the signs and wonders God had done among the Gentiles through them.*
>
> (Acts 15:12)

And again:

> *So we all agreed to choose some men and send them to you with our dear friends Barnabas and Paul*
>
> (Acts 15:25)

It's a detail, but perhaps a significant one. It might well be that Luke reverts to the old way of describing the two – Barnabas and Paul – because that's how the church in Jerusalem viewed the partnership. Barnabas was one of theirs, originally sent out by them, Paul was not. Perhaps they still viewed Barnabas as the senior partner. Perhaps we shouldn't read too much into this, because sandwiched between those two descriptions of 'Barnabas and Paul', Luke reverts to 'Paul and Barnabas' once again (Acts 15:22). But it's a thought worthy of consideration.

And it's not that Barnabas, the older man of the two, ever became Paul's subordinate. But in their working relationship, Paul gradually became more prominent, as he took a greater speaking role.

-    -    -    -    -

The transition began as Paul experienced an anointing of the Holy Spirit that enabled him to confront Elymas the sorcerer. As Luke tells us that Paul was 'filled with the Holy Spirit' (Acts 13:9) during this encounter, there's no mention of Barnabas experiencing that anointing, and no complaint from him about it either.

We mustn't presume too much from silence, but it's undeniable that a shift was happening.

This transition of Paul into apparent prominence happened 'on the road'. The role shift emerged.

It happened in response to mission.

And it happened without fanfare or warning. And from that moment on, nothing would ever be quite the same.

Everything was changing for Paul. And everything was changing for Barnabas at the very same time.

-    -    -    -    -

Was Barnabas taken aback by what happened? Perhaps, as the wizard spat out words of derision at the missionary pair, words were already forming in Barnabas' mind: as the leader up until now, perhaps he was quickly formulating a response.

# But then Paul spoke up. And Barnabas didn't interrupt.

Some see the fact that Barnabas allowed Paul to take the lead here as a risky step of faith, creating an opportunity for Paul to step up to the plate of initiative and leadership:

> *Barnabas was willing to take the risk of letting Paul speak on Cyprus and Paul responded to the challenge of a false teacher, even calling a curse on him ... which caused the proconsul of the region to believe teaching of the Lord ... Barnabas would never know how far Paul advanced unless he tested him. Paul found that he could minister in the power of the Holy Spirit ... Barnabas was willing to suppress his need to be the leader on every occasion for the good of the organization and his mentee's development.*[5]

If it was a risk, Barnabas took it. He'd taken a risk on Paul before, back in Jerusalem. And just as he was glad when he saw the grace of God at work in Antioch, I imagine he was glad this time too, as he witnessed God so powerfully using Paul.

# When you don't have to be first, you're free to celebrate when others are blessed.

You don't have to have their gifts, experiences or encounters.

\-    \-    \-    \-    \-

Handing over the reins of primary leadership can be a relief. At last, you're no longer carrying the weight of final responsibility. You're not the focal point for criticism from your opponents, as Barnabas would later find out when Paul was violently attacked by a mob, but he was not.

But there can be some internal challenges that go with the transition. A sense of failure can sneak up on you.

Have you been replaced because you made some mistakes, either because you weren't up to the task, or because your successor is more gifted than you?

And then you no longer have such a say in strategic decision making. You may contribute to the conversation, but somebody else has the casting vote. When the team was Barnabas supported by Paul, decisions like where they travelled to, their strategy in mission and who travelled with them had Barnabas taking the initiative, even if all of these matters had perhaps been decided collectively. But now increasingly Paul would have had the final say-so. If anyone doubts that this can create real tension, let's realise that ultimately Paul and Barnabas would split up because of a serious and deep conflict over strategy and personnel. Once upon a time, there would have been no issue because Barnabas would most likely have made the call as the senior partner.

And then there's an issue of respect and honour. When things go well, people tend to applaud the senior leader who has taken them to success. Those team members who have contributed to the success are often overlooked.

Whatever was involved in taking a more secondary role, Barnabas was not only willing, but probably was delighted as young Saul became bold Paul. Perhaps that's what he intended all along.

-       -       -       -       -

Mary Gordon has written a prayer for those whose work is secondary, or even invisible:

> *For those who paint the underside of boats, makers of ornamental drains on roofs too high to be seen; for cobblers who labor over inner soles; for seamstresses*

*who stitch the wrong side of linings; for scholars whose
research leads to no obvious discovery; for dentists
who polish each gold surface of the fillings of upper
molars; for sewer engineers and those who repair
water mains; for electricians; for artists who suppress
what does injustice to their visions; for surgeons whose
sutures are things of beauty. For all those whose work
is for Your eyes only, who labor for Your entertainment,
or their own, who sleep in peace or do not sleep in
peace, knowing that their effects are unknown.*

*Protect them from downheartedness
and from diseases of the eye.*

*Grant them perseverance, for the sake of Your love,
which is humble, invisible and heedless of reward.*[6]

Amen to that.

# Thirteen:
## WEAR RIPPED CLOTHES

'In Lystra there sat a man who was lame. He had been that way from birth and had never walked. He listened to Paul as he was speaking. Paul looked directly at him, saw that he had faith to be healed and called out, "Stand up on your feet!" At that, the man jumped up and began to walk.

When the crowd saw what Paul had done, they shouted in the Lycaonian language, "The gods have come down to us in human form!" Barnabas they called Zeus, and Paul they called Hermes because he was the chief speaker. The priest of Zeus, whose temple was just outside the city, brought bulls and wreaths to the city gates because he and the crowd wanted to offer sacrifices to them.

But when the apostles Barnabas and Paul heard of this, they tore their clothes and rushed out into the crowd, shouting: "Friends, why are you doing this? We too are only human, like you. We are bringing you good news, telling you to turn from these worthless things to the living God, who made the heavens and the earth and the sea and everything in them. In the past, he let all nations go their own way. Yet he has not left himself without testimony: he has shown kindness by giving you rain from heaven and crops in their seasons; he provides you with plenty of food and fills your hearts with joy." Even with these words, they had difficulty keeping the crowd from sacrificing to them.

Then some Jews came from Antioch and Iconium and won the crowd over. They stoned Paul and dragged him outside the city, thinking he was dead. But after the disciples had gathered round *him, he got up and went back into the city. The next day he and Barnabas left for Derbe.*

*They preached the gospel in that city and won a large number of disciples. Then they returned to Lystra, Iconium and Antioch, strengthening the disciples and encouraging them to remain true to the faith. "We must go through many hardships to enter the kingdom of God," they said. Paul and Barnabas appointed elders for them in each church and, with prayer and fasting, committed them to the Lord, in whom they had put their trust. After going through Pisidia, they came into Pamphylia, and when they had preached the word in Perga, they went down to Attalia.' - Acts 14:8-25*

'Remembering that I'll be dead soon is the most important tool I've ever encountered to help me make the big choices in life. Almost everything - all external expectations, all pride, all fear of embarrassment or failure - these things just fall away in the face of death, leaving only what is truly important.' - Steve Jobs[1]

'Vanity and pride are different things, though the words are often used synonymously. A person may be proud without being vain. Pride relates more to our opinion of ourselves, vanity to what we would have others think of us.' - Jane Austen[2]

The host looked nervous.

Speaking for a week at a Bible conference, I'd been accommodated at a local bed and breakfast.

The room was nice: clean, bright and with a very comfortable bed. And the lady who owned the place was welcoming and kind. Picking me up for the evening meeting, the conference organiser looked at me quizzically.

'Is your accommodation okay?' he ventured, obviously hesitant.

'It's delightful, thanks,' I affirmed, realising that this was more than polite small talk. He was worried.

His concerned frown softened. He sighed with relief.

I wondered why he seemed so anxious, and asked.

It turns out that, the previous year, the main speaker had obviously been less happy with his accommodation, and had said so in a very public and shocking manner. Pausing during preaching on the first night of the event, he told the crowd that the arrangements for housing the conference speakers were inadequate and dishonouring, and that he insisted that the whole speaker team, himself obviously included, be moved to a nearby hotel. He would pay the entire bill for the accommodation himself, he declared, to the obvious embarrassment of the red-faced organisers who agreed to comply; the next day, everyone was relocated.

Using words like hospitality and honour, the speaker demonstrated something very simple: he had forgotten basic principles of respect and kindness, and had become something of a legend. A little god.

In his own mind.

-    -    -    -    -

There had been some triumphs and disappointments for Barnabas and Paul as they continued their travels.

A sail to Pamphylia had led to John Mark deciding to
return home to Jerusalem, a decision that obviously
disappointed Paul deeply. From there, they headed for
Pisidian Antioch, where Paul preached powerfully in the
synagogue (Acts 13:16-41). The sermon went so well that
they were invited to share again the following week, with
a trail of interested congregants following them after the
service was dismissed. They encouraged the crowds, and
then the next weekend, when the Sabbath came around
again, the sight that awaited them at the synagogue was
staggering - Luke says that 'almost the whole city gathered
to hear the word of the Lord' (Acts 13:44). Success creates
jealousy; the Jews in the city were incensed and became
abusive, and so Paul and Barnabas were blunt, telling
the Jews that they were 'turning' now to the Gentiles.

The Gentiles were glad.

The Jews, unsurprisingly, were upset, stirred up trouble, and
that led to the pair being unceremoniously ejected from the
city. They responded by holding a little ceremony of their own,
which involved shaking the dust off their sandals (Acts 13:51).

In Iconium, they headed for the synagogue once again, and the
response was great - numbers of Jews and Gentiles believed.
Opposition came from the Jewish quarter once again, but Paul
and Barnabas held on, and there were great miracles, signs
and wonders performed through their ministry. Opposition
continued, the city was divided between those for and those
against, a plot to stone them both was hatched, and so they fled
to Lystra and Derbe, still preaching as they went (Acts 14:1-7).

In the remote town of Lystra, another stunning miracle
happened as a disabled man was instantly healed and
walked, to the amazement of the citizens (Acts 14:8-10).

But in trying to make sense of this supernatural event, the Lycaonians[3] turned to their own traditions and myths for a solution. These were people who cherished an ancient legend that Zeus and Hermes had once come to the hill country disguised as mortals, looking for hospitality and a room for the night. They looked in vain for a welcome, visiting no fewer than a thousand homes, but to no avail. They were shunned – nobody would open their home, until finally, a poor elderly couple, Philemon and Baucis, threw open their humble home and gave the visitors a feast, even though they themselves had so little.

They were to be richly rewarded, because the gods transformed their cottage into a temple, and the couple became the resident priest and priestess. And the rewards continued. When they died, they were immortalised as a great oak and a great linden tree. But the homes where the gods had been refused were destroyed.[4]

The chastened, fearful Lycaonians were determined not to make the same mistake again, and so when two men arrived who apparently had the power of God with them, the locals mistakenly thought that the men themselves were the powerful gods Zeus and Hermes, come back for a return visit. And nobody wanted to lose their homes. So they rolled out an idolatrous red-carpet welcome (Acts 14:11-13).

Perhaps Paul and Barnabas didn't immediately realise what was happening. Luke records that the locals were speaking to each other in their own dialect, which the missionary pair would not have understood. But if they were suspicious that something was amiss, their suspicions were confirmed when a priest of the local Zeus cult showed up with a sacrifice and some woollen wreaths, symbols of reverence and honour. It was all going horribly wrong.

THERE ARE NO ORDINARY PEOPLE

As soon as Paul and Barnabas realised what was happening, they took radical action to stop it immediately. Genuinely alarmed at the blasphemous idolatry that was about to take place, they dashed into the crowd, ripping their clothes as they did.

# Why the clothes ripping?

In biblical culture, one would tear the clothes on one's back as a sign of mourning, distress, or to protest a blasphemy.[5]

Tragically, the high priest did the same thing when Jesus stood before him. It was a dramatic act that gave the baying crowd a very powerful message: this man is a blasphemer.

> *Again the high priest asked him, 'Are you the Messiah, the Son of the Blessed One?'*
> *'I am,' said Jesus. 'And you will see the Son of Man sitting at the right hand of the Mighty One and coming on the clouds of heaven.'*
> *The high priest tore his clothes. 'Why do we need any more witnesses?' he asked. 'You have heard the blasphemy. What do you think?'*
> *They all condemned him as worthy of death. Then some began to spit at him; they blindfolded him, struck him with their fists, and said, 'Prophesy!' And the guards took him and beat him.*
>
> (Mark 14:61-65)

As the missionary pair tore their clothes, their dramatic act put a stop to the misdirected worship immediately. Then Paul and Barnabas made it absolutely clear that, far from being gods, they were just human like everyone else. Herod Antipas had proclaimed himself a god – and judgment had come upon him as a result (Acts 12:21-23).

Perhaps none of us are ever going to face the temptation of being worshipped by people who want to slay cattle and decorate us with flowers.

# But we can very easily lose sight of the truth that we are mere mortals.

There are no ordinary people - but those who live extraordinary lives of everyday heroism never graduate from the status that earth dwellers all share: we are human beings. But we can so easily forget that truth.

\-     \-     \-     \-     \-

It can happen to leaders. Not many good people survive greatness. Over years of ministry, I've met many good men and women - people of passion, integrity, focus and with a genuine calling. Their character has not been perfect, but they have been wholesome, kind and generous. And then something happens that slowly, gradually changes them. It's not that they are derailed by temptation, or spoiled by outright, overt sin, but instead they become casualties of their own prominence. People begin to notice and applaud them; they are respected, even revered, because of their gifts.

Slowly and surely, goodness fades out of their lives - they become demanding, feeling as though they are special and should be served. Their initial confidence distils into ugly arrogance. Some with strong, assertive leadership skills morph into bullies who have the ultimate weapon that they use to badger and intimidate people with - their insistence that God is on their side, and is telling them to take authority.

Success - 'greatness', if I can describe it like that - is a heady experience, and can create headstrong people.

Trusted and respected as a figurehead and a key leader in the Early Church, Barnabas' goodness survived greatness.

# Whenever we are celebrated or elevated, let's make sure that we have not left goodness behind.

Because, leaders or not, it can happen to all of us.

We forget we're human.

We forget that we're just humans when we insist that we're unfailingly right all the time.

When we become obsessed with the human fragility of others, but ignore our own weaknesses.

When we push ourselves beyond reasonable limits physically and emotionally, ignoring our limitations and mortality.

When we hear that someone has failed badly, and we insist that we could never fall in the way that they have.

When we justify every decision by saying that God has told us to do what we're doing, as if we have a virus-free online connection to heaven.

When we refuse to listen to the opinions of others, and quickly write them off because they disagree with our perspective.

When we assume that we're right, and speak with a haughty authority about everything, even in matters way beyond our expertise.

It happens, and it happened to me. I was shocked when I heard about the hotel incident. But then I discovered that I could easily succumb to something similar, which I need to confess.

-        -        -        -        -

Even in sharing what I'm about to say, there's a risk of being misunderstood. But here goes. Some years ago, I was invited to speak at a large conference. Already booked to be somewhere else, I jokingly replied that I could fulfil the invitation, but they'd need to send a plane to pick me up and drop me back the same day if it was to happen. Imagine my surprise when the conference organiser, who had a friend who owned a private jet, said, 'Done. We're glad you can come.' Too embarrassed to refuse, the day came when I drove my car into a field, a jet landed and I was whisked to the other end of the country to address the conference. On my arrival, a car was waiting at the private airport, and when we got to the conference centre, I was whisked into a green room where people were waiting with fruit, snacks and drinks. I was being treated like a VIP. And here's the part I didn't want to confess: I really liked it. It was a heady feeling. In the end, I asked the conference host if I could just leave the green room and walk around and chat with people, and get my feet back on the ground.

# Applause of any kind is seductive, and can be difficult to resist.

But you don't have to be treated like a VIP in order to momentarily lose your grasp of your own humanity. All we have to do is to start thinking that we are above the rules and principles that everybody else has to adhere to: that we are a special case.

-        -        -        -        -

Bill Hybels is the dynamic leader of the 20,000-strong Willow Creek Community Church in the USA. He is widely respected and applauded, not least because, with all his success, he presents himself in a human, humble manner. But that hasn't been an easy posture to maintain:

> One evening I stopped by the church just to encourage those who were there rehearsing for the spring musical. I didn't intend to stay long, so I parked my car next to the entrance. After a few minutes, I ran back to my car and drove home.
>
> The next morning I found a note in my office mailbox. It read: A small thing, but Tuesday night when you came to rehearsal, you parked in the 'No Parking' area. A reaction from one of my crew (who did not recognize you until after you got out of the car) was, 'There's another jerk parking in the "No Parking" area!' We try hard not to allow people – even workers – to park anywhere other than the parking lots. I would appreciate your cooperation, too. It was signed by a member of our maintenance staff ...
>
> [This man's] stock went up in my book because he had the courage to write me about what could have been a slippage in my character.
>
> And he was right on the mark. As I drove up that night, I had thought, I shouldn't park here, but after all, I am the pastor. That translates: I'm an exception to the rules. But that employee wouldn't allow me to sneak down the road labeled 'I'm an exception.'
>
> I'm not the exception to church rules ... or any of God's rules. As a leader, I am not an exception: I'm to be the example. According to Scripture, I am to live in such a way that I can say, 'Follow me. Park where I park. Live as I live.'
>
> That's why we all need people like my staff member to hold us accountable in even the small matters. Because when we keep the minor matters in line, we don't stumble over the larger ones.

*Just when I was starting to think,*
*I'm an exception, somebody on our staff*
*cared enough to say, 'Don't do it, Bill, not*
*even in one small area.' That's love.*[6]

\-       \-       \-       \-       \-

There's a sad postscript to the story about the speaker
who felt he and his fellow preachers were not being
treated appropriately with their accommodation.

He didn't realise that, while he was criticising the standard of
the little bed and breakfast, the owner of that establishment
was seated in the congregation. Not normally a churchgoer, she
had chosen that night to go to the conference, to find out what
it was all about, only to hear her business criticised publicly.

And then the speaker had promised to pay the bill
for the relocation of the whole preaching team.

To add insult to injury, the cheque never arrived.

\-       \-       \-       \-       \-

Paul and Barnabas were tested to the extreme as
some wanted to elevate them as gods. Considering the
rejection that they'd experienced, it must have made
for a nice change to be so warmly welcomed.

As it turned out, the adulation was fickle. It usually
is. After the pair had stopped the worship service
in their honour, some troublemakers arrived.

*Even with these words, they had difficulty keeping*
*the crowd from sacrificing to them. Then some*
*Jews came from Antioch and Iconium and won*

*the crowd over. They stoned Paul and dragged*
*him outside the city, thinking he was dead.*

(Acts 14:18-19)

The sudden change in attitude was almost unbelievable,
as those who had wanted to elevate Paul and Barnabas
as gods turned on them simply because a group of rabble
rousers had arrived from Antioch and Iconium. The crowd
of would-be worshippers was suddenly convinced that
the apostolic pair were anything but gods, and, despite the
miracles that had been done, they turned on Paul (having
just applauded him as the chief speaker) and stoned
him. This was a very serious assault. He was obviously
rendered unconscious by the lynch mob, because they
dragged him out of the city and thought he was dead.

One moment Paul was a god, and the next he was a
target, a potential victim of a mob bent on killing him.

It's nice to be encouraged, appreciated,
affirmed and even honoured.

But let's remember this when others speak too well of others,
or when we're tempted to take an inflated view of ourselves:

We're fragile, incomplete, flawed creatures and we're
in possession of something that should remind us
of what we really are - and that is a pulse.

# We're human. So keep wearing ripped clothes.

# Fourteen:
## STICK TO YOUR STORY

'From Attalia they sailed back to Antioch, where they had been committed to the grace of God for the work they had now completed. On arriving there, they gathered the church together and reported all that God had done through them and how he had opened a door of faith to the Gentiles. And they stayed there a long time with the disciples.' – Acts 14:26-28

'When Cephas came to Antioch, I opposed him to his face, because he stood condemned. For before certain men came from James, he used to eat with the Gentiles. But when they arrived, he began to draw back and separate himself from the Gentiles because he was afraid of those who belonged to the circumcision group. The other Jews joined him in his hypocrisy, so that by their hypocrisy even Barnabas was led astray.

When I saw that they were not acting in line with the truth of the gospel, I said to Cephas in front of them all, "You are a Jew, yet you live like a Gentile and not like a Jew. How is it, then, that you force Gentiles to follow Jewish customs?"' – Galatians 2:11-14

'Certain people came down from Judea to Antioch and were teaching the believers: "Unless you are circumcised, according to the custom taught by Moses, you cannot be saved." This brought Paul and Barnabas into sharp dispute and debate with them. So Paul and Barnabas were appointed, along with some other believers, to go up to Jerusalem to see the apostles and elders about this question.

*The church sent them on their way, and as they travelled through Phoenicia and Samaria, they told how the Gentiles had been converted. This news made all the believers very glad. When they came to Jerusalem, they were welcomed by the church and the apostles and elders, to whom they reported everything God had done through them.*

*Then some of the believers who belonged to the party of the Pharisees stood up and said, "The Gentiles must be circumcised and required to keep the law of Moses."*

*The apostles and elders met to consider this question. After much discussion, Peter got up and addressed them: "Brothers, you know that some time ago God made a choice among you that the Gentiles should hear from my lips the message of the gospel and believe. God, who knows the heart, showed that he accepted them by giving the Holy Spirit to them, just as he did to us. He did not discriminate between us and them, for he purified their hearts by faith. Now then, why do you try to test God by putting on the necks of Gentiles a yoke that neither we nor our ancestors have been able to bear? No! We believe it is through the grace of our Lord Jesus that we are saved, just as they are."*

*The whole assembly became silent as they listened to Barnabas and Paul telling about the signs and wonders God had done among the Gentiles through them.' – Acts 15:1-12*

*'Then the apostles and elders, with the whole church, decided to choose some of their own men and send them to Antioch with Paul and Barnabas.' – Acts 15:22*

*'Paul and Barnabas remained in Antioch, where they and many others taught and preached the word of the Lord.' – Acts 15:35*

It was one of the highlights of the youth camps that I attended as a new Christian. Clutching cups of steaming hot chocolate, we would gather late in the evening to sing songs, pray prayers and share what we called 'testimony time'. Giving a testimony was simple: you walked to the front of the meeting, took the microphone and shared an answer to prayer, a Bible verse that had been relevant and meaningful or a conversation that had been purposeful: the testimony time reminded us that God was alive and active, and we were participants in His great plans.

Were some of the 'testimonies' a little silly, exaggerated, even foolish? Of course. But those testimonies did so much to energise my fledgling faith.

Preaching tells the epic blockbuster that is the story of God; our occasionally thin little testimonies connected us to that big story. Our sharing put flesh on the bones of the gospel for us. They inspired us, challenged us, stirred us. We clapped and cheered each other; our smiles were wide and genuine; our hearts warmed.

As Mark Batterson says:

> Hearing a testimony is the way I borrow faith from others. Sharing my testimony is the way I loan my faith to others. If we aren't sharing testimonies, we're cutting off circulation to the body of Christ. Part of the body becomes numb. And we don't just lose feeling in that part of the body. If it is starved of testimony long enough, it will eventually die. So we need to celebrate what we want to see more of. Our testimonies of what God has done in the past become prophecies of what God will do in the future. If you start sharing testimonies of miraculous conversions to Christ, you'll see more of those miracles happen. The same is true of healing or deliverance or provision. It's like inhaling pure oxygen. It not only regenerates faith but also charges the atmosphere of a church so that it becomes highly combustible.[1]

The stories certainly challenged us to
fresh commitment to Jesus.

\-       \-       \-       \-       \-

Paul and Barnabas returned home to Antioch (not Pisidian
Antioch, but rather the Antioch where they had served
together in leadership in the church that had given them an
apostolic commission, where they had been 'committed to
the grace of God'). The church in Antioch was their 'sending'
church, and so it was only right that they took time to report
back and give an account of their work. Imagine being at
that meeting as the two recounted stories of struggles and
faith, of new converts and angry mobs, of warm welcomes
and hurried getaways. High-ranking Roman officials had
come to faith; smear campaigns had been mounted.

# God was the real hero of their report.

Their stories were shared not only with their fellow
leaders but with the whole congregation, which gathered
especially so that they could hear about their adventures.

Barnabas and Paul were able to share how God had
strengthened them to stick to their story, their good
news story, in the face of opposition and persecution.

But even as they gathered and celebrated, a new,
unexpected threat was heading their way.

Peter was heading to town, perhaps just passing through.
This would surely cement the relationship between
the Christians in Antioch and Jerusalem further.

But his visit was about to be marred, spoiled by
another group of visitors who were heading towards
Antioch, bringing division and trouble with them.

Remarkably, Peter would end up loosening his
grip on grace, under pressure from that bullying
band who were about to hit town.

And he'd be joined in his compromise by the man who
had been so astute at seeing grace at work, who had
urged believers everywhere to continue in the grace
of God. Sadly, under pressure, he would capitulate to
legalism, and threaten the health and future of the entire
congregation at Antioch. What was about to happen could
undo all the good work he had done there, because he
was about to deviate from the story of amazing grace.

# He should have stuck to the story, but he did not.

Barnabas.

-     -     -     -     -

Every strength has a composite weakness.

The person who loves to serve people can
become a driven slave, exhausted and never
convinced that they've done enough.

The kind, compassionate soul can be targeted by
manipulative grabbers, and their tender heart exploited.

The honest, authentic type can unwittingly create bruises,
because they just can't stand anything fake or duplicitous,
and so they just have to say exactly what they think.

Barnabas had so many great strengths.

He was a bridge person, willing to believe the best.
But the bridge can be opened to dangerous people,
and, in believing the best, he suspended any sense of suspicion
and opened the way to highly destructive predators.

Barnabas liked harmony; he wanted opposites to live together
in harmony. That meant that when legalists showed up, he tried
to link them up with the grace people. New wine, old wineskins.

He was open-hearted too, eager to give people a fair
hearing, and was always respectful of their views. And
that meant that in his open-heartedness, he was able
to be duped by some very bad ideas indeed; blinded
by his care and concern for the people, he nodded his
head in agreement with their ideas rather too quickly.

He was a sensitive soul, and would go out of his way to
avoid offending people. But maybe he went a mile too
far out of his way. Some people need to be offended.

Barnabas was a great listener, eager to give people a full hearing
before he reached a verdict. But he could have ended up fence-
sitting, endlessly deliberating and playing it safe while he did so.

Barnabas wanted peace.

# But peace cannot be bought at any price.

Meanwhile, a virus of error entered the church at
Antioch. Incredibly, through Peter and Barnabas.

And Paul was enraged about it.

Barnabas was unwilling to upset and offend those visitors to Antioch. And his reluctance caused Paul to be very upset indeed.

We need to be willing to upset people. We just need to know who, when and why to cause the upset.

- - - - -

I so wanted him to be perfect, or almost.

But Barnabas had feet of clay. Perhaps it's helpful to know that he was not a perfect portrait of encouragement and consistency. In the latter part of his ministry at Antioch, he seriously let Paul down. Barnabas was a good man, but not superman. Yet he still played such a vital role in the Church.

# There's hope for us all.

Luke does not describe Barnabas' capitulation under pressure in the book of Acts. We have to fill in the blank from what Paul wrote to the Galatians, and so piece the sad story together.

As we've read, Peter - Paul calls him 'Cephas' in this context - was visiting the Antioch church. On arrival, he joined in with the 'love feasts', which were attended by both Jewish and Gentile converts and during which communion was shared. But that beautiful portrait of unity was about to be shattered.

The other visitors from Jerusalem arrived.
And that's when the trouble began (Gal. 2:11-14).

The visiting delegation, who insisted that they came on the authority of the apostle James (which they probably did not), were demanding that the church withdraw from eating meals with the Gentile converts. This episode illustrates just how difficult the Early Church found it to disentangle itself from separatist Jewish legalism. Later the Jerusalem Council, writing to the believers in Antioch, described troublemakers who 'went out from us without our authorisation and disturbed you, troubling your minds by what they said' (Acts 15:24).

Perhaps Peter and Barnabas didn't know that the 'credentials' were likely false, but, for whatever reason, they buckled under pressure and slowly drew back into ritual separation. The language used doesn't suggest a sudden action, but rather a slow, systematic withdrawal. However, the effect was still devastating. Others followed their leaders, and soon Peter and Barnabas found themselves spearheading an aloof, separatist group.

The church in Antioch was split right down the middle as a result. Jewish converts here. Gentile converts there.

Stop and look.

This was the man who had celebrated the grace of God working wonderfully among the Gentiles.

He had been their first pastor yet he had started to withdraw from them, which must have been so terribly hurtful and divisive.

Barnabas had been part of the wider mission to the Gentiles, establishing converts in Galatia.

But at this point he was acting in complete contradiction to all that he knew and all that he had worked for.

He was acting like a hypocrite, according to Paul's own strong words. In fact, Paul uses a term that comes from the theatre, *hypokrites*, and it means to wear a mask or play a part. This was not a thoughtless mistake on the part of Peter and Barnabas - they were violating their convictions about the grace message, which was being overturned.

The Gentile converts had been told that they were fully accepted, but now the behaviour of their first leader was contradicting that truth. Little wonder Paul was so angry, and rightly so. Religious freedom and the unity of the entire Church was at stake.

# Religion can hijack us where sin doesn't succeed.

This sad saga also demonstrates that Barnabas - as Paul says with a shaking of his head, 'even Barnabas' - could get it wrong. We all can. Helpfully, Paul was at hand and didn't hold back from a solid rebuke for them both. And Paul was right.

So why did Barnabas do it?

Perhaps Barnabas had started to worry about his and Paul's mission to the Gentiles. Some scholars say that John Mark may have left the mission field not because he was afraid, but because he disagreed with Paul's strategy of taking the gospel outside of the synagogues, speaking in marketplace situations and engaging pagan philosophers.

Later on, Paul was to refuse John Mark as a team member - is it possible he did that because John Mark was too conservative for such a radical mission, and Barnabas had been affected by that conservative but also legalistic thinking too?

We can speculate at best.

What we do know is that fear was behind this move by Peter, Barnabas and the Jewish Christians in Antioch. Perhaps they feared physical violence, although both Barnabas and Peter had stayed true to the story when they were threatened before.

Perhaps they were terrified that they would offend the spurious delegation, and fear of causing that upset made them withdraw.

Barnabas loved people, and loved people to be happy.

That's a noble ambition, but it must have its
limits, because the blunt truth is this:

We won't make everyone happy.

# The gospel story is not available for revision.

It declares the uniqueness of Christ, as the only way. Jesus refuses to be aligned with a pantheon of god-choices.

It invites those who would follow Jesus to
experience genuine holiness, with standards that
fly in the face of the current cult of tolerance.

While it never sanctions a ranting Church, it does call
for a confident Church, able to declare truth, through
word and deed, in the marketplace of ideas.

It is a message that exposes the hollowness of legalism,
where people strive to please God through keeping petty
rules and regulations that are dreamed up by humans,
and invites sinners to accept that they become saints
by simply accepting God's love, mercy and grace.

It's the old, old story, ever relevant, ever
new. Let's stick to that story.

For a while, Peter, and even Barnabas, surrendered that story,
and began to embrace a law-laced myth, a distorted tale.

Thankfully, however, Paul didn't spare their blushes.
They saw sense. And came back to the story once more,
defenders of it again, fuelled with renewed vigour.

-      -      -      -      -

Okay, it's confusing. Follow this with me carefully if you will.

In Antioch (according to Galatians), Barnabas and
Peter withdrew from eating with Gentiles.

In Acts, Luke describes a visit of some legalistic Christians
from Judea to Antioch. We can't be certain, but some
scholars believe the 'visitors' described in Galatians 2 and
the 'certain people' of Acts 15 are the same group, and
the two texts are describing the same disastrous visit.

But here's the quandary.

Paul describes Barnabas as a fellow capitulator who
buckled under pressure, with Peter, as we've seen.

But then Luke says that Barnabas joined Paul
in confronting the legalists, coming 'into sharp
dispute and debate with them' (Acts 15:2).

The fight gets ugly, leading to a decision to send Paul and
Barnabas to Jerusalem to consult with the leadership there.
During that Council gathering, Peter argued for full inclusion
of the Gentiles into the Church. Paul and Barnabas described
how God blessed their mission work among the Gentiles.
James spoke. A letter was drafted, insisting that the legalistic
'visitors' had no authority from Jerusalem at all, and set out
some guidelines to facilitate full integration of the Gentiles
into the Church without overly complicated demands.

Paul and Barnabas were commissioned to
take the letter back to Antioch.

If I'm following this correctly, here's what happened:

Peter and Barnabas lost their grip on the story in Antioch.

Paul went ballistic and confronted them.

Peter, chastened, returned to Jerusalem.

Barnabas changed his mind (it's good to do that when you're wrong) and joined Paul in the fight against the divisive visitors, and then accompanied Paul on the trip to the Jerusalem conference, and together they spoke up for grace and freedom.

Stick to the story.

# And, if you've lost your grip on grace, then have a change of heart and mind.

Barnabas did, and once again became a powerful advocate for freedom.

# Fifteen:
# KNOW THAT EVERYTHING IS BROKEN

*'Some time later Paul said to Barnabas, "Let us go back and visit the believers in all the towns where we preached the word of the Lord and see how they are doing." Barnabas wanted to take John, also called Mark, with them, but Paul did not think it wise to take him, because he had deserted them in Pamphylia and had not continued with them in the work. They had such a sharp disagreement that they parted company. Barnabas took Mark and sailed for Cyprus, but Paul chose Silas and left, commended by the believers to the grace of the Lord.' - Acts 15:36-40*

*'From Paphos, Paul and his companions sailed to Perga in Pamphylia, where John left them to return to Jerusalem.' - Acts 13:13*

*'My fellow prisoner Aristarchus sends you his greetings, as does Mark, the cousin of Barnabas. (You have received instructions about him; if he comes to you, welcome him.)' - Colossians 4:10*

*'Get Mark and bring him with you, because he is helpful to me in my ministry.' - 2 Timothy 4:11*

'I think I would have liked to meet and work with Barnabas. I am sure he would have made me feel that I had a contribution to make.

He would have brought out the best in me.
But Paul? I am not so sure!' - Dick France[1]

'Ever since Barnabas had retrieved Paul
from Tarsus to help with the ministry
in Antioch, their teamwork had been
charmed with grace.' - R. Kent Hughes[2]

'I am rough, boisterous, stormy, and altogether
warlike. I am born to fight against innumerable
monsters and devils. I must remove stumps
and stones, cut away thistles and thorns,
and clear the wild forests' - Martin Luther[3]

It sounds like a negative comment, a pessimistic,
even cynical notion from somebody who is a
casualty of repeated disappointments.

Everything is broken.

That's my most recent life lesson. I've been sharing that
little three-word sentence with fellow leaders everywhere
I go. Some seem shocked, worried that nearly forty
years in ministry has robbed me of hopefulness.

Others are relieved, liberated to know that it's okay to affirm
the truth: in this world, nothing is perfect. Everyone is
broken. Some humans are in the recovery process, slowly,
gradually being transformed by the Holy Spirit, becoming
what Christ wants them to be. But none have arrived.
There are no marriages, churches, people, organisations,
leaders, followers or denominations that are completely
whole: all are broken, and will be this side of Jesus' coming,

when the kingdom will be fully established, and wholeness will then come and finally banish our brokenness for good.

That means that I don't have to hunt for the perfect church, or look to serve in what seems to be the perfect denomination or movement, only to discover the flaws and then feel the need to move on to look for something better.

I don't have to be surprised and devastated when that fellow Christian leader is deeply unkind, or unholy.

I don't bow before the brokenness, resigned to it, but I can play my part in building something, yet resting in the knowledge that the work will only be fully completed, in it, in them or in me, when the Lord Jesus comes.

# Everything is broken.

All heroes are flawed, with *One* obvious exception.

The reality of the conflict between those two great men, Paul and Barnabas, together with the significant gaff when Barnabas fell prey to the bullying Judaisers back in Antioch, shows this stark truth. Yes, Barnabas' feet were made of clay.

The relationship between those two travelling companions was dynamic, supernatural, brave and world changing. But it was broken too, because it was a partnership between two broken men in a broken world. And it was about to split apart, permanently, as a result of what was more than a mild disagreement. This was not a calm discussion, but a sharp, full-on argument, a blazing row.

The word Luke uses to describe their spat means violent action or emotion. Thankfully, Luke doesn't gloss over the raw facts; to do so would simply fuel naive idealism. Instead, he shows us the painful reality of a fall out between two men who had changed the world together.

- - - - -

It's a sad picture that I've seen too many times. Christian leaders who have been friends and colleagues for many years, in some cases have even grown up together, come to a place where conflict creates an irreparable rift, and they part with animosity. Usually it is not just their veteran relationships that suffer, but the work that, under God, they have built together is weakened or even divided too.

Paul and Barnabas were back in Antioch, having played a vital part in the Council of Jerusalem, where the issue of Gentile circumcision had been settled. Grace had triumphed and won the day - on that day, at least.

Barnabas and Paul had probably spent the winter months working together in Antioch, and now, with the coming of spring, and the opening of travel routes by land and sea once more, Paul felt that it might be good for the pair to revisit the churches established on their first journey together. This was not pioneer evangelism, but a visit to strengthen the new Christians, and see how they were doing.

Barnabas agreed to the idea, but the impasse came when the discussion moved on to deciding who should accompany them. Barnabas opted for his relative, John Mark, who had dropped out of the team's earlier missionary journey in Pamphylia. Luke uses a word that gives some insight to Mark's departure; he hadn't just left, but he'd 'stood aloof' or 'turned away' from them. Paul was not about to see a repeat of that behaviour, and said so.

Again, a close look at the Greek in this text shows that Barnabas wanted to give Mark 'another shot', a limited second chance, but Paul was wanting to build an ongoing team, and taking John Mark would have been a permanent move in his eyes.

# Barnabas voted for grace, leniency.

Paul obviously saw Barnabas as a soft touch, whereas history had proven that to be wrong.

Despite his temporary lapse in Antioch, Barnabas had gone on to speak out boldly in the turbulent row about the Gentiles. And years earlier, he had willingly broken ranks with the leadership in Jerusalem in his insistence that they welcome Saul into their ranks.

Perhaps that's the irony behind this tragic conflict: Paul was unwilling to extend grace, and came into conflict with the very man who had shown him grace when nobody else wanted to take that risk, Barnabas.

Paul had defended grace in Jerusalem, but didn't seem willing to extend mercy to John Mark in Antioch. Lloyd Ogilvie comments:

> Paul had fought and won one of history's most crucial battles over the Gentile converts. He was not able, however, to apply the same truth to his relationship with John Mark.[4]

In his reluctance to give a further ministry opportunity to John Mark, Paul fought with the man who had given him a further ministry opportunity, after ten silent years in Tarsus, when the invitation came from Barnabas to team up in Antioch.

And so the dynamic duo divided.

-        -        -        -        -

Luke doesn't offer a verdict on the fight: deciding that one man was right and the other wrong. Perhaps it's telling, though, that the church in Antioch 'commended'

Paul and Silas, but nothing was said about any commendation of Barnabas and Mark (Act 15:40). A possible vote in favour of Paul being in the right, if they were voting.

But then John Mark would ultimately be accepted by Paul again, becoming a right-hand man to him. Barnabas was right about Mark's potential; the man gave us the second Gospel. There's a vote for Barnabas; they're even.

I confess that I lean towards supporting Barnabas. I love his tender-heartedness, and his gift of being able to see a person rather than an incident of failure. And perhaps even this argument points us to Barnabas' great skill as a mentor. He had played such a significant role in nurturing Paul into confidence. He had coached Paul to the place where, when challenged back in Cyprus by that demonised wizard, Paul had spoken up boldly.

And when there was conflict, Paul, the mentoree, felt able to argue with his former tutor – a sign that Barnabas had schooled the young man well.

The conflict was obviously caused by a significant personality clash.

# Barnabas' strength was his love for people; Paul was a tireless defender of truth.

Both had their weaknesses. If they could have stayed together, what a wonderful complement they might have continued to be to each other.

In our defence of truth, let's never become hard faced and stern, quickly dismissing those who don't believe our version of the gospel.

In our defence of people, let's never sanction constantly bad behaviour or doctrinal error because we're unwilling to graciously and gently confront.

And, when we have a fight - not if, because conflict is a healthy reality of life - let's fight nicely. Because broken Paul and broken Barnabas did not.

-        -        -        -        -

It seems that the fight between the two generated more heat than light.

There's no record of them praying together, asking God to help them as they found themselves in the unfamiliar territory of conflict. The book of Acts is full of prayerful decisions, choices made after worship and fasting, but it seems that their row and parting were fuelled by hurt rather than any sense of God's direction and wisdom.

Shared prayer is hard to accomplish when we disagree, but it may be the best thing to do, when we stop talking heatedly to each other - to pause for a while to talk with God.

There was also no attempt to seek any help from a mediator in the fuss. That's odd too, because the pair had served as peacemakers just shortly before in the Council of Jerusalem. They knew what consultation and facilitated conversation could achieve, even in the most contentious situations.

# But they handled this disagreement by themselves, and they handled it badly.

And so it ended.

Barnabas stomped off with cousin John Mark
and headed for Cyprus again, and Paul recruited
Silas and made his way to Syria and Cilicia.

Both men continued in the work. But not together.

Sad as the sight is, perhaps there's a vital principle to notice.

Sometimes, while reconciliation is what we might
hope for, we have to concede that some friendships,
marriages and church affiliations have to come to an
end. The damage is too great, trust has been so eroded,
betrayal has run so deep that there's no way back.

This is not about bitterness or a lack of forgiveness. I can
offer forgiveness in a situation, but that doesn't mean that
the partnership or relationship will continue as it was.

Both men continued faithfully in their
ministry. But they did so apart.

-        -        -        -        -

Although the team split, some think that Barnabas and
Paul did repair their relationship eventually, although
that idea is implied rather than stated. Later Paul would
write to the church in Corinth and speak with respect and
warmth about his historical ministry with Barnabas:

> is it only I and Barnabas who lack the
> right to not work for a living?

(1 Cor. 9:6)

And Paul mentions Barnabas, ironically in connection
with John Mark, in Colossians (Col. 4:10).

While not attempting to rush to bring something good
out of something bad, God did redeem the fight. Now
there were two missionary ventures, not one.

Barnabas and John Mark.

Paul, Silas, Timothy and Luke. Silas was better
suited for the second missionary journey, because
he was probably a Roman citizen, like Paul.

Paul was able to reach new, unreached cities,
because Barnabas was taking care of the works
that had previously been established.

And Paul seemed to have learned from the debacle of the
defection of John Mark, insisting later that it is not wise
to 'lay hands suddenly' on unproven, untested people
(1 Tim. 3:10; 5:22). And the kindness and tender care that Paul
showed to young, 'timid' Timothy, demonstrated that he did
develop a greater sense of empathy towards others who
were less confident and even less courageous than himself.

While some have concluded that God orchestrated this parting,
I think that's a rather overly positive conclusion. I don't think
God arranged and organised a fight. But He did redeem it.

# Fight fair. It will be an extraordinary sight.

And if we've been involved in conflicts that were messy and
ugly, if there's nothing more that we can do now, let's ask God to
do what only He can do, and bring redemption out of that pain.

# Sixteen:
## PLAN YOUR FUNERAL

*'Barnabas took Mark and sailed for Cyprus, but Paul chose Silas and left, commended by the believers to the grace of the Lord.'*
*- Acts 15:39-40*

'The following conversation took place at Timothy's funeral. His memorial service affected people deeply. Mourner after mourner shared powerful stories about the way the 45-year-old man had touched their lives. "That was wonderful," one man exclaimed. "When I die, I want the exact same service. The same music, the same Bible readings, the same words."
Another man put a hand on his shoulder. "Our church doesn't do cookie cutter funerals," he said. "If you want a funeral like this one, then you are going to have to live a life like Timothy between now and when you die."' – Dan Dobson[1]

'I want words at my funeral.
But I guess that means you need
life in your life.' – Markus Zusak[2]

It's been said that when Barnabas sailed away from Paul, he
sailed away from recorded history. And that's true, because
Luke records nothing further about Barnabas. All we know
is that he went to Cyprus with John Mark, where Barnabas
is traditionally honoured as the founder of the Church.

It seems that Barnabas continued in his travels, because Paul
continued to mention him, but we don't have any details.

There is a tradition that Barnabas became first bishop of
Milan, and that he was martyred in AD 55, which would
be around six years after the fateful fight with Paul. (Others
say it happened as late as twenty years after that date.)[3]

The story goes that when he was preaching in Syria
and Salamis with extraordinary success, Barnabas was
attacked whilst he was debating in the synagogue.
He was dragged out, tortured terribly and then stoned
to death.[3] Some say he was burned as well.

It is alleged that his remains were discovered 400 years
later, after a vision given to an archbishop helped identify
his grave. A copy of Matthew's Gospel was buried at his side.
A chapel of the St Barnabas Monastery still sits on that site.

What a legacy he lived and left behind too.

I love that John Ortberg describes this kind, warm man, who
really lived and died, as an everyday hero. It is because of
the way he ceaselessly urged the early disciples and apostles
to persevere that the gospel message has travelled so far.

So let's plan our funerals. I'm not talking song selection, flower preferences, funeral directors that are pre-paid or even the sandwiches that they'll snack on after the service.

I'm talking about how people will remember and reflect upon our lives.

# The impact we made, the love we shared.

Let's live in such a way that, in the humdrum unfolding of everyday life, we, with all our flaws, live a head-and heart-turning example of what Jesus is really like.

In a world where so many are scrambling up the ladder, let's resist the urge to make a name for ourselves, and instead allow others to tag us with a nickname that reflects our kindness.

Rather than endless grabbing, let's give hilariously, knowing that as we give out, we give up to God.

Let's go when we're called to go, but stay when it's less exciting to be solid and faithful.

Knowing that fear is the vandal of life, God grant us trust and peace when fear comes hunting.

Generally, let's believe the best, rather than scouring to confirm that our worst suspicions are true.

Being heard is priceless, and rare. Let's intentionally listen.

Christians aren't just people who know how to behave: they are apprentices who are being changed from the inside, with renewed minds and open-heart surgery from the Holy Spirit. Today, be filled and co-operate with the surgeon.

Invest in losers. Go hunting as a talent spotter. Bet on people who have long odds against them.

Today is the first day of the unfolding forever that
is ours. The horizon stretches into infinity, but
today won't come around again. Spend it well.

Satan has a forked tongue. Beware.

Don't clamour for first place. Serve, and know that in
serving and becoming the least, therein lies true greatness.
And, if greatness and applause comes, keep wearing
the torn clothes of humility and humanity. In a world
where everything is being broken, but will one day be
redeemed and restored, stick to the story, that big story.

-     -     -     -     -

Tradition has it that after Barnabas died, an old
friend and family member came and privately
interred his body, and then carried news of his
death to Paul, who was in Ephesus at the time.[4]

The identity of that man is significant, and speaks
volumes about the departed hero that was Barnabas.

It was John Mark.

# Epilogue:
## IT'S NEVER TOO LATE

It was one of those life skills that I never learned at school.

School told me how many wives Henry VIII had, helped me glean information about Australia's mining industry and even taught me the French word for 'station', but nobody told me anything about that one thing you don't believe will ever happen when you're young, yet it happens to every human on the planet.

And that is how to grow older well.

Lately, I've been lamenting this glaring gap in my education, because, despite my insistence that there's been a terrible mistake on my birth certificate, old is what I'm getting. Others are noticing, and have been observing it for a while.

I was offered over-sixties discounts in restaurants before I turned fifty. And then a repair man came to our house, met me and then later met my wife Kay, and asked her to pass on a message to her dad – referring to me. My lovely, and apparently youthful, wife didn't correct the misunderstanding, but called up the stairs, 'Daaaad'.

I walked into a clothing store usually frequented by younger men. As I pushed the door and stepped in, the pre-adolescent chap wearing skinny jeans that were probably impeding his circulation looked up and said, 'Hello sir. Looking for something a little more trendy, are we?'

And just yesterday, when Kay and I checked in at the airport, a grinning airline person made the comment: 'So, travelling with your daughter today, are you?' Hilarious. Not.

So, finally conceding that the clock is not just ticking, but racing, I've been grateful for one man who has been something of a distant tutor not only when it comes to ageing, but on living beautifully. His real name is James, but, for years now, everyone has called him Shotgun; I have no idea why. He lives in Oklahoma, which may provide a clue. Such an impact has he made upon me, I have written about him elsewhere.[1] Forgive the repetition, but Shotgun is worth it.

Shotgun is ninety-four years old now, and has lived most of his life without wanting Jesus to be part of it. When he was twelve, he went to a church, and told God that if He was real, then he'd like to meet Him. Nothing happened. He describes the experience as being one of the most disappointing of his life. He walked out and decided to ignore God for the rest of his days, and lived the rough and ready life of an oil worker, often drunk, getting into fights and occasionally being thrown in jail.

It went on that way for some seven decades. His wife was the love of his life, and so, when they were both in their mid-eighties and she announced that she thought they should go to church, he agreed. A short while later, Shotgun's wife became very ill. He was granted a rare privilege: one night, they lay awake for most of the night, reminiscing, reviewing their lives together, whispering words of love. In the morning, he awoke to find that she was not in their bed. She had got up, made her way to their sitting room, where he found her, sitting up against the couch, quite dead. Six months later, Shotgun walked into his pastor's study and said, 'I'm ready'. They knelt down together on the floor, and Shotgun asked Jesus if they could reconnect.

Reconnect they have, and the result is beautiful.

I am going to Oklahoma again this week, and looking forward to it, but it won't be the same, because Shotgun won't be there. He has business elsewhere, and I'll miss him. He's shown me what growing old, not just graciously, but beautifully, can look like.

Whenever we've met, he has always brought cheer to my soul. Always tearful and tender, he is loved by everyone in his church, and for good reason. He arrives for services early and makes them coffee. He's still full of questions, and shows the rare ability for a man of his age to be able to grow and change. But what's most noticeable about Shotgun is his kindness, which is just quietly outstanding. In short, he cares. Encourages. Serves. Learns. Extraordinary is what he is.

But this week, he's away on other business, in heaven. I just got news today that he has passed away, but I talk about him in the present tense, because Shotgun still is. He's absent from the body, present with the Lord and, if there's coffee in heaven (which surely there must be), he's probably serving it right now, along with that warm, winsome smile. I'll miss that smile, but not for too long.

Who knows? Perhaps he's bumped into a jovial, bearded chap called Barnabas. I think they'd get along rather well.

Good night, Shotgun. See you in the morning. Resurrection morning.

Thanks for being a great tutor. May I grow older with grace like you did.

And thanks for living out this truth: when it comes to living the ordinary life heroically, it's never too late.

# Endnotes

## PREFACE: NOBODY IS ORDINARY (BUT NOT EVERYTHING IS AWESOME)

[1]Katrina Kenison, *The Gift of an Ordinary Day* (New York: Grand Central Publishing, 2009) Kindle edition

[2]Carla Robertson, 'Permission to live an ordinary life' blog posted 7 January 2014 on livingwildandprecious.com [Accessed 30 March 2015]

[3]George Eliot, *Middlemarch* (London: Penguin Classics, 2003) Kindle edition

[4]Dick France, 'Barnabas, Son of Encouragement', *Themelios*, Vol 4, Issue 1, Jan/Sep 1978, p6

[5]Helen Keller cited in Charles L. Wallis, *The Treasure Chest* (New York: HarperCollins, 1965) p240

[6]Generous Church, 'Week 1: The Secrets of Generosity', p2 of www.generouschurch.com/uploads/generosity_sunday_school_wk_1.pdf [Accessed 30 March 2015]

[7]Zelda la Grange, *Good Morning, Mr Mandela* (London: Penguin, 2014) Kindle edition

[8]Bill Bryson, *One Summer: America, 1927* (New York: Doubleday, 2013)

[9]Morgan Lee, 'Nancy Writebol: Ebola is a Spiritual Battle', *Christianity Today*, 15 October 2014, article available at www.christianitytoday.com [Accessed 30 March 2015]

[10]David McCullough cited in B. Brown, 'Wellesley High grads told: "You're not Special"', *The Swellesley Report*, 5 June 2012, article available at theswellesleyreport.com [Accessed 30 March 2015]

[11]Kyle Worley, 'Celebrating the "Ordinary"' blog posted 24 July 2013 on cbmw.org [Accessed 30 March 2015]

[12]Catherine Porter, 'Shelagh was here - an ordinary, magical life', *Toronto Star*, 16 March 2012, article available at www.thestar.com [Accessed 30 March 2015]

[13]Robin Gallaher Branch, 'Barnabas: Early Church leader and model of encouragement', *In die Skriflig*, Vol 1, Issue 2, 2007, p297

[14]William Martin, *The Parent's Tao Te Ching: Ancient Advice for Modern Parents*. Taken from www.goodreads.com/quotes/505843 [Accessed 31 March 2015]

## CHAPTER ONE: BECOME A SUPERMODEL

[1]J.W. Packer, *The Acts of the Apostles* (Cambridge: Cambridge University Press, 1966) p43

[2]Taken from www.goodreads.com/quotes/129294 [Accessed 31 March 2015]

[3]Ronald Heifetz, *The Practice of Adaptive Leadership* (Cambridge: Harvard Business Press, 2009) p78

[4]Taken from www.goodreads.com/quotes/950858 [Accessed 31 March 2015]

[5]Taken from www.goodreads.com/quotes/355391 [Accessed 31 March 2015]

[6]Jonny Miller, 'Insight into Will Smith's Philosophy' blog posted 17 January 2013 on jonnymiller.co/blog [Accessed 31 March 2015]

[7]Taken from www.goodreads.com/quotes/306084 [Accessed 31 March 2015]

[8]David Soren, 'Death at Kourion', *Island Jewels* (Biblical Archaeology Society, 2008) p3. Available at s3.amazonaws.com/presspublisher-do/upload/2891/Island_Jewels_Understanding_Ancient_Cyprus_and_Crete.pdf [Accessed 31 March 2015]

[9]John B. Polhill, *Paul and His Letters* (Nashville: Broadman & Holman Publishers, 1999) p39

[10]Marc Freedman, 'Don't Leave a Legacy; Live One', *Harvard Business Review*, 11 December 2012, article available at hbr.org [Accessed 31 March 2015]

[11]Susan V. Bosak, 'What is Legacy?', Legacy Project, available at www.legacyproject.org/guides/whatislegacy.html [Accessed 31 March 2015]

[12]John Donne, Henry Alford (ed), *The Works of John Donne* (London: John W. Parker, 1839) p291

[13]Quoted in John C. Maxwell, *Developing the Leader Within You* (Nashville: Thomas Nelson, 1993) p4

[14]John R.W. Stott, *The Message of Ephesians* (Downers Grove: Inter-Varsity Press, 1989) Kindle edition

## CHAPTER TWO: DON'T MAKE A NAME FOR YOURSELF

[1]George Matthew Adams quoted in John C. Maxwell, *25 Way to Win with People* (Nashville: Thomas Nelson, 2005) p37

[2]Mark Twain quoted in Keith Johnson, *The Confidence Makeover* (Shippensburg: Destiny Image Publishers, 2006) p37

[3]John C. Maxwell, *Encouragement Changes Everything* (Nashville: Thomas Nelson, 2008) p13. Used by permission of Thomas Nelson

[4]Albert Schweitzer cited in Larry Chang, *Wisdom for the Soul* (Washington: Gnosophia Publishers, 2006) p403

[5]John C. Maxwell, *Winning with People Workbook* (Nashville: Thomas Nelson, 2004) p37

[6]Nathan Tan, *The Forgetful Gentleman* (San Francisco: Chronicle Books, 2013) p114

[7]Dr Larry Crabb and Dr Dan Allender, *Encouragement: The Key to Caring* (Grand Rapids: Zondervan, 1990) Kindle edition

## CHAPTER THREE: GIVE UP

[1]Robin Gallaher Branch, *ibid*, p305

[2]Charles Dickens, *A Christmas Carol* (London: Bradbury & Evans, 1858) p2

[3]Chip Ingram, *The Genius of Generosity* (Generous Church, 2010) Kindle edition

[4]Gordon MacDonald, *Generosity: Moving Toward a Life that is Truly Life* (Generous Church, 2009) Kindle edition

[5]Aesop quoted in Larry Chang, *ibid*, p136

[6]Andy Stanley, *How to Be Rich* (Grand Rapids: Zondervan, 2013) Chapter Seven, Kindle edition

[7]Peter Burgo, 'Those Impious Galileans', *Alliance Life*, December 2009, article available at www.cmalliance.org/alife/those-impious-galileans [Accessed 2 April 2015]

[8]For more on *liberalitas*, see Andy Stanley, *ibid*

[9]Andy Stanley, *ibid*

[10]Gordon MacDonald, *ibid*

[11]Miroslav Volf, *Free of Charge* (Grand Rapids: Zondervan, 2006) p114

[12]Christian Smith and Hilary Davidson, *The Paradox of Generosity* (New York: Oxford University Press, 2014) p2

[13]*Ibid*, p12

[14]Charles Dickens, *ibid*

[15]Andy Stanley, *ibid*

## CHAPTER FOUR: STAY HOME SOMETIMES

[1]Jon Acuff, *Quitter* (Brentwood, TN: Lampo Press, 2011) Kindle edition

[2]Eugene H. Peterson, *A Long Obedience in the Same Direction* (Downers Grove: Inter-Varsity Press, 2000) p17

[3]Acts 14:14 is the first time Barnabas is referred to as an apostle

[4]Eugene H. Peterson, *The Pastor* (New York: HarperCollins, 2011) p135

[5]Richard Selzer, *Mortal Lessons* (San Diego: Harcourt, 1996) pp45-46. Reprinted by permission of Georges Borchardt, Inc. on behalf of the author

## CHAPTER FIVE: BE VERY, VERY AFRAID

[1]Taken from www.goodreads.com/work/quotes/1466917 [Accessed 2 April 2015]

[2]Taken from www.goodreads.com/quotes/46179 [Accessed 11 April 2015]

[3]Frank Herbert, *Dune* (London: Gateway, 2010) Kindle edition. Used by permission of G.P. Putnam's Sons, an imprint of Penguin Publishing Group, a division of Penguin Random House LLC

[4]Taken from www.goodreads.com/quotes/453737 [Accessed 2 April 2015]

[5]Max Lucado, *Fearless* (Nashville: Thomas Nelson, 2009) p5. Used by permission of Thomas Nelson

[6]Taken from 'Nelson Mandela: 11 Inspirational quotes to live your life by', *The Independent*, 6 December 2013, article available at www.independent.co.uk [Accessed 2 April 2015]

[7]Frank Furedi, *Culture of Fear* (London: Continuum, 2002) xii. Reprinted by permission of Bloomsbury Publishing Plc.

[8]Max Lucado, *ibid*, pp176-177

[9]David Woolner, 'Overcoming the Great Recession Will Take Courage, Not Fear' 1 June 2010, article available at www.rooseveltinstitute.org [Accessed 7 April 2015]

[10]Clive Stafford Smith, 'Fear is the Worst', *Intelligent Life*, September/October 2012, article available at moreintelligentlife.com [Accessed 7 April 2015]

[11]Max Lucado, *ibid*, p11

## CHAPTER SIX: GENERALLY, BELIEVE THE BEST
[1]Stephen Kendrick and Alex Kendrick, *The Love Dare*
(Nashville: B&H Publishing Group, 2008) p33

[2]Taken from www.goodreads.com/quotes/35464 [Accessed 7 April 2015]

[3]Taken from www.goodreads.com/quotes/1198373 [Accessed 7 April 2015]

[4]John Sloane, *The Barnabas Way* (Colorado Springs: Waterbrook Press, 2003)
pp42-43

[5]For further reading: Richard Bauckham, 'Barnabas in Galatians',
*Journal for the Study of the New Testament*, Vol 1, Issue 2, March 1979, p62

## CHAPTER SEVEN: FOR GOD'S SAKE, LISTEN
[1]Dr Paul Tournier cited in Charles R. Swindoll, *Growing Strong in the Seasons of Life*
(Grand Rapids: Zondervan, 1983) p69

[2]Taken from www.goodreads.com/quotes/18897 [Accessed 7 April 2015]

[3]Taken from www.goodreads.com/quotes/52591 [Accessed 7 April 2015]

[4]Taken from www.goodreads.com/quotes/442589 [Accessed 7 April 2015]

[5]Taken from www.goodreads.com/quotes/522585 [Accessed 7 April 2015]

[6]Taken from www.quotes.net/quote/4336 [Accessed 7 April 2015]

[7]Rachel Naomi Remen, 'Just Listen' article available at www.livinglifefully.com/flo/
flobejustlisten.htm [Accessed 7 April 2015]

[8]Michael P. Nichols, *The Lost Art of Listening* (New York: Guilford Press, 1995) p1.
Reprinted with permission of the Guilford Press

[9]Takeshi Takazawa cited in Earl Creps, *Reverse Mentoring* (John Wiley & Sons,
2008) p97

## CHAPTER EIGHT: UNDERGO OPEN-HEART SURGERY
[1]Taken from www.goodreads.com/quotes/74099 [Accessed 7 April 2015]

[2]Vincent Nichols, 'Archbishop of Westminster: Full Sermon', *BBC News*, 21 May
2009, available at news.bbc.co.uk/1/hi/uk/8061710.stm [Accessed 7 April 2015]

[3]Taken from www.goodreads.com/quotes/94470 [Accessed 7 April 2015]

[4]Robin Gallaher Branch, *ibid*, p317

[5]Winston S. Churchill, speaking to the House of Commons on the Munich
Agreement, 3 October 1938

[6]Craig Brown, 'Good golly, the brolly has been jolly significant', *The Daily Mail*,
8 October 2009, article available at www.dailymail.co.uk [Accessed 8 April 2015]

[7]Taken from www.newworldencyclopedia.org/entry/William_Wilberforce
[Accessed 8 April 2015]

[8]Marc Malkin, 'Keira Knightley's Teenage Years', *E!*, article available at www.eonline.com/news/589927/keira-knightley-s-teenageyears-i-was-a-goody-two-shoes [Accessed 8 April 2015]

[9]Taken from www.thefreedictionary.com/do-gooder [Accessed 8 April 2015]

[10]Taken from www.urbandictionary.com/define.php?term=goody+two+shoes&def id=1163357 [Accessed 8 April 2015]

[11]William Barclay, *William Barclay's Daily Study Bible*, Acts 11:22-26, taken from www.studylight.org/commentaries/dsb/view.cgi?bk=ac&ch=11 [Accessed 8 April 2015]

[12]R. Kent Hughes quoted by John Barnett in his sermon 'Grace-Energized Kindness', 19 August 2007, available at www.dtbm.org/sermon/grace-energized-kindness/ [Accessed 8 April 2015]

[13]Taken from www.roman-empire.net/emperors/nero.html [Accessed 8 April 2015]

## CHAPTER NINE: INVEST IN THE BIGGEST LOSERS

[1]Some Bible translations use 'to' instead of 'from'

[2]Quoted in Cory Miller, 'Invest in People and They Will Invest in You' blog posted 13 February 2010 on corymiller.com [Accessed 8 April 2015]

[3]Taken from www.lifeoptimizer.org/2007/10/10/43-most-insightful-friendship-quotes/ [Accessed 8 April 2015]

[4]*Ibid*

[5]*Ibid*

[6]Warren W. Wiersbe, *The Wiersbe Bible Commentary: New Testament* (Colorado Springs: David C. Cook, 2007) p360

## CHAPTER TEN: TUNE IN TO MIDDLE C

[1]Dallas Willard, *The Divine Conspiracy* (New York: HarperCollins, 1998) xvii

[2]Donald McCullough, *The Trivialization of God* (Colorado Springs: NavPress, 1995) p13

[3]*Ibid*

[4]Michael Griffiths, *Cinderella with Amnesia* (Leicester: Inter-Varsity Press, 1975)

[5]Gareth Higgins, *How Movies Helped Save My Soul* (Lake Mary, FL: Relevant Books, 2004) pp191-194

[6]Ted Koppel, commencement speech at Duke University, Durham, North Carolina, 10 May 1987, taken from archive.mrc.org/mediawatch/1989/watch19890401.asp [Accessed 9 April 2015]

[7]Donald McCullough, *ibid*

[8]*Ibid*

[9]This famous story is variously quoted, including in Donald McCullough, *ibid*, p66

## CHAPTER ELEVEN: BEWARE OF SLURRED SPEECH

[1]C.S. Lewis, *The Screwtape Letters* (New York: HarperOne, 2009) Preface, Kindle edition © copyright CS Lewis Pte Ltd 1942

[2]Taken from www.goodreads.com/quotes/176384 [Accessed 9 April 2015]

[3]M. Scott Peck, *People of the Lie* (New York: Simon & Schuster, 1983) p183

[4]Basil Jackson cited in Kersten Beckstrom, *Topical Encyclopedia of Living Quotations* (Minneapolis: Bethany House Publishers, 1982), p41

[5]Taken from Martin Luther's hymn *A Mighty Fortress Is Our God* (1529)

[6]Jay Sharbutt, 'Cauldron Boils Over Geraldo's "Devil Worship"', *Los Angeles Times*, 27 October 1988, article available at articles.latimes.com/1988-10-27/entertainment/ca-449_1_devil-worship [Accessed 9 April 2015]

[7]msnbc.com staff, 'Devil in the details', *NBC News*, 22 February 2012, article available at usnews.nbcnews.com [Accessed 9 April 2015]

[8]*Ibid*

[9]*Ibid*

[10]Cited in John P. Newport, *Life's Ultimate Questions* (Dallas: Word Publishing, 1989) p185

[11]The Barna Group, 'Most American Christians Do Not Believe that Satan or the Holy Spirit Exist', 2009, article available at www.barna.org/barna-update/faith-spirituality/260 [Accessed 9 April 2015]

[12]Anthony Buzzard, 'Satan, the Personal Devil', article available at focusonthekingdom.org/articles/satan.htm [Accessed 9 April 2015]

[13]Martin Luther, *A Mighty Fortress is Our God*, c. 1529

[14]See Acts 13:9. The name 'Paul' would have been more appropriate as he brought the gospel to the Gentiles because they were more accustomed to this name.

## CHAPTER TWELVE: GO FOR THE SILVER MEDAL

[1]Ray Williams, 'Why Do We Have an Obsession with Winning?', *Psychology Today*, 4 August 2012 , article available at www.psychologytoday.com/blog/wired-success/201208/ [Accessed 9 April 2015]

[2]David McCullough quoted in B. Brown *ibid*

[3]John Sloane, *ibid*

[4]Tom Stafford, 'Olympics: Why winning a bronze medal beats silver', *BBC*, 10 August 2012, article available at www.bbc.com/future/story/20120810-olympic-lessons-in-regret [Accessed 9 April 2015]

[5]Orlando Rivera, 'Mentoring Stages in the Relationship between Barnabas and Paul' May 2007, available www.regent.edu/acad/global/publications/bpc_proceedings/2007/rivera.pdf [Accessed 9 April 2015]

[6]Mary Gordon, 'Six Prayers', *God is Love: Essays from Portland Magazine*, Brian Doyle (ed), (Minneapolis: Augsburg Books, 2003) pp29-30

## CHAPTER THIRTEEN: WEAR RIPPED CLOTHES

[1]Taken from www.goodreads.com/quotes/427317 [Accessed 10 April 2015]

[2]Jane Austen, *Pride and Prejudice* (Melbourne: Penguin, 2013) Chapter Five, Kindle edition

[3]Lystra was in the eastern region of Lycaonia, which is why its inhabitants are often referred to as Lycaonians

[4]Ovid, *Metamorphoses: Books 6-10* William S. Anderson (ed) (Oklahoma: University of Oklahoma Press, 1972) p390 (note: in Latin, Hermes is Mercury and Zeus is Jupiter)

[5]Here are some more biblical examples: Genesis 37:29,34; 2 Samuel 1:11-12; 1 Kings 21:27; 2 Kings 2:11-12; Job 1:20; Judges 11:34-35; Esther 4:1

[6]Bill Hybels, 'But I'm Not an Exception', *Leadership Journal*, Spring 1988, p37, article available at www.christianitytoday.com/le/1988/spring/8812037.html [Accessed 10 April 2015]

## CHAPTER FOURTEEN: STICK TO YOUR STORY
[1]Mark Batterson, *The Grave Robber* (Grand Rapids: Baker Books, 2014) pp150-151

## CHAPTER FIFTEEN: KNOW THAT EVERYTHING IS BROKEN
[1]Dick France, *ibid*, p5

[2]R. Kent Hughes, *The Church Afire* (Wheaton: Crossway, 1996) Kindle edition. Used by permission of Crossway, a publishing ministry of Good News Publishers

[3]Martin Luther, cited in Philip Schaff, *History of the Christian Church, Volume VII* (Grand Rapids: CCEL, 2010) Kindle edition

[4]Lloyd J. Ogilvie quoted in Wayne Jackson, 'The Separation of Paul and Barnabas', *Christian Courier*, article available at www.christiancourier.com/articles/813 [Accessed 10 April 2015]

## CHAPTER SIXTEEN: PLAN YOUR FUNERAL
[1]Quoted by Dan Dobson, 'Thanksgiving Message', blog posted 15 November 2012 on discoveringdan.blogspot.co.uk [Accessed 10 April 2015]

[2]Taken from www.goodreads.com/quotes/48579 [Accessed 10 April 2015]

[3]John Fleetwood, *The Life of Our Blessed Lord and Savior Jesus Christ* (Philadelphia: Garretson, 1874) p600

[4]*Ibid*

## EPILOGUE: IT'S NEVER TOO LATE
[1]Adrian Plass and Jeff Lucas, *Seriously Funny* (Milton Keynes: Authentic Media, 2010)

Courses and seminars

Waverley Abbey College

Publishing and media

Conference facilities

# Transforming lives

CWR's vision is to enable people to experience personal transformation through applying God's Word to their lives and relationships.

Our Bible-based training and resources help people around the world to:
• Grow in their walk with God
• Understand and apply Scripture to their lives
• Resource themselves and their church
• Develop pastoral care and counselling skills
• Train for leadership
• Strengthen relationships, marriage and family life
and much more.

Our insightful writers provide daily Bible reading notes and other resources for all ages, and our experienced course designers and presenters have gained an international reputation for excellence and effectiveness.

CWR's Training and Conference Centres in Surrey and East Sussex, England, provide excellent facilities in idyllic settings – ideal for both learning and spiritual refreshment.

**CWR** Applying God's Word
to everyday life and relationships

CWR, Waverley Abbey House,
Waverley Lane, Farnham,
Surrey GU9 8EP, UK

Telephone: **+44 (0)1252 784700**
Email: **info@cwr.org.uk**
Website: **www.cwr.org.uk**

Registered Charity No. 294387
Company Registration No. 1990308